William Woollcombe

Sermons on Various Subjects

William Woollcombe

Sermons on Various Subjects

ISBN/EAN: 9783744743143

Printed in Europe, USA, Canada, Australia, Japan

Cover: Foto ©Lupo / pixelio.de

More available books at **www.hansebooks.com**

SERMONS

ON

VARIOUS SUBJECTS.

By the Rev. WILLIAM WOOLLCOMBE, M. A.
Late PREBENDARY of EXETER,
And RECTOR of EAST-WORLINGTON and LAWRENCE-CLYST.

PRINTED AND SOLD BY TREWMAN AND SON;
SOLD ALSO BY MESSRS. RIVINGTON,
ST. PAUL's CHURCH-YARD,
LONDON.

M,DCC,XCVIII.

ADVERTISEMENT.

THE Editors of the following Discourses, cannot permit their publication, without expressing their regret for its long delay; and assuring the Subscribers that it has been occasioned by circumstances, which, with the utmost solicitude for dispatch, could not possibly be prevented. They wish also, in justice to the memory of their Author, to observe, that they were not written with the remotest idea of public inspection; otherwise they would, in a literary view, have possessed greater pretensions to the very respectable and liberal patronage with which they have been honoured.

JULY 2, 1798.

ADVERTISEMENT.

The Editors of the following work cannot permit their publication, without their regret for its long delay to the Subscribers, that it was occasioned by circumstances, which could not be prevented, to the memory of who are not

A LIST OF SUBSCRIBERS

TO THE

SERMONS

OF THE

Late Rev. WILLIAM WOOLLCOMBE.

A.

DOWAGER Countefs Albermale, *two Copies*
Lady Harriet Ackland, Picton-Houfe, *two Copies*
Lady Arnefton, Edinburgh, *two Copies*
Lady Afhburton, *two Copies*
Lady Aubrey
Mr Abbot, Exeter
Rev. Mr. Abrahams, Crewkerne
Hugh Ackland, Efq. *two Copies*
William Adams, Efq. M. P. Plympton, *ten Copies*
Mr. Adams, Totnes, *two Copies*
Mr. Jofeph Adams, Lifkeard
Thomas Adkin, Efq. *two Copies*

Thomas Allen, Efq. London, *two Copies*
Nathaniel Allen, Efq. London, *two Copies*
Rev. Mr. Alford, Heal-Houfe
Rev. T. Alfop
Mrs. Anderdon, Bath
Mrs. Sufan Anderdon, Ditto
Rev. John Andrew, Powderham
Mrs. Arbouin, Bath
Mrs. W. Armftrong
Mifs Arfcott, Okehampton
Mr. Afh, St. Germains
Mr. Edward Afh, Briftol
Mrs. Mary Afhley, Bath, *two Copies*
―― Atwood, Efq. Ditto
―― Warden of All Souls
Anonymous

B.

Her Grace the Duchefs of Buccleugh, *two Copies*
Lord Bridport, *two Copies*
Lady Bridport, *two Copies*
Lady Georgiana Buckley, *two Copies*
Lady Blantyre, Scotland
Hon. Mifs Stuart Blantyre, Ditto
Rev. Michael Babbs, Lyme
Andrew Bain, Efq. Lainftow, Hants

Sir

Sir George Baker, Bart. M. D. *two Copies*
Dr. Thomas Baker, Loventor, *ten Copies*
Mr. John Baker, Briftol, *two Copies*
Rev. Slade Baker, Ditto, *two Copies*
Mr. John Baker, Eaft-Worlington, Devon
Mr. T. Baker, Weft-Worlington, Ditto
Mifs Ball, Bath
Mifs Ball, Mevagiffey, Cornwall
Rev. Mr. Ball, Winfrith
Rev. R. W. Bampfylde, Poltimore
Mrs. E. Bampfylde, Bath
William Barbor, Efq. Fremington, Devon, *four Copies*
Mrs. F. Baril, Winchefter-ftreet, London
Charles Baring, Efq. Courtland, *twenty Copies*
John Baring, Efq. M. P. Mount-Radford, *ten Copies*
Sir John Barrington, Swanfton, Ifle of Wight, *two Copies*
Mr. Bare, Puddington, *two Copies*
Colonel Barnard, Bideford
James Barnard, Efq. Crowcombe, Somerfet
Mrs. Barnard, London
Rev. Robert Cary Barnard, Withersfield, Suffolk
Mrs. Barnard, Ditto
Rev. Charles Drake Barnard
Mr. G. Barne, Tiverton
Archdeacon Barnes, Exeter, *two Copies*
Mrs. Barnes, Ditto, *two Copies*

Mr. Barnes, Chrift-Church College, Oxon
Mr. Barnes, Exeter College, Ditto
James Barrow, Efq. London, *two Copies*
Rev. William Barter, Timfbury, Prebendary of Wells, *four Copies*
Rev. Robert Bartholomew, Exeter
Subdean Barton, Exeter, *ten Copies*
Mrs. Barton, Durrant
Mifs C. Baffet, Tehiddy-Park
John Pollexfen Baftard, Efq. Kitley, *fifteen Copies*
Edmund Baftard, Efq. Sharpham, *ten Copies*
—— Bate, Efq. Royal Hofpital, Greenwich
William Batterfby, Efq. Briftol
Mr. Bathifcomb, Windfor
Mrs. Poole Bathurft, Bath, *two Copies*
—— Batt, Efq. New-Hall, Wilts, *two Copies*
Mrs. Batt, Ditto
Benjamin Baugh, Efq. Briftol, *two Copies*
Mrs. Bailey, Exeter
Rev. Edward Baynes
Rev. R. Bawdon, Warkley, Southmolton
Mifs Bearde, Penzance
Mr. Beck, Frenchay, *two Copies*
—— Bedford, Efq. Barrifter at Law, London
Rev. William Bedford, Mary-Tavy, Devon
Rev. Finney Belfield, Primleys, Devon, *twenty Copies*

Mr.

Mr. Belitha, Cornwall
Mrs. Bellamy
—— Benham, Esq.
Mr. William Bennet, Organist, Plymouth
Mr. John Bennet, Merchant, Ditto
Rev. Mr. Benson, London
Rev. Edmond Benson
Mrs. Benson
Rev. George Bent, Sandford
Mr. Berjew, Bristol, *two Copies*
Mr. Bethell
Miss Bickford, Dunsland, *two Copies*
—— Biddulph, Esq.
Richard Bingham, Esq. Melcombe, Dorset, *ten Copies*
Mrs. Bingham, Ditto, *ten Copies*
Miss Bingham, Ditto, *four Copies*
Miss Leonora Bingham, Ditto, *four Copies*
Lieutenant-Colonel Bingham, *two Copies*
Dr. Bingham, Gaddesdon, Hants, *two Copies*
Rev. Peregrine Bingham
Rev. William Bingham, *two Copies*
Rev. George Bingham, Pimperne, *two Copies*
Miss Bingham, Ditto, *two Copies*
Mrs. Blackall, Exeter, *two Copies*
Henry Blackall, Esq. Ditto
Dr. Blackall, Ditto

Mr. T. Blackall, Ditto
Rev. S. Blackall
Mrs. Blackman, London
Mrs. M. Blackman, Ditto
Mrs. Blackmore, Hanſden, Herts
Mrs. Blagrove, Bath
Rev. John Blake, Rector of Shoreditch
Rev. Mr. Blake, Crewkerne
Joſeph Bland, Eſq. London, *two Copies*
—— Blicke, Eſq South Lambeth
Mrs. Bloſſett
Richard Blundell, Eſq. Tiverton, *two Copies*
Mrs. Boger, Smitham
Miſs Bond, St. James's-ſquare, Bath.
Mrs. Bonfoy, Ditto
Mr. Thomas Bonville, Briſtol
Mrs. Borlaſe, Cornwall
Major Bothwell, Royal North Britiſh Dragoons
Mrs. John Bourge, Caſtle-Cary, Somerſet
E. F. Bourke, Eſq. Fort-Houſe, Briſtol, *two Copies*
Mrs. Bourke, Ditto, *two Copies*
Miſs Bourke, Ditto, *two Copies*
Miſs H. Bowdler
Mrs. Bower, Ewerne, Dorſet
Rev. William Liſle Bowles, M. A. Donhead, Wilts
Mrs. Boyce, Bath

Mrs.

Mrs. Bracheu, Ditto
—— Brand, Efq. Topfham, *four Copies*
John Brathwayte, Efq. Bath, *two Copies*
Edward William Bray, Efq. Taviftock
Rev. Mr. Brereton, Canon Refidentiary, Litchfield, Leicefter
Rev. Mr. Brereton, Exeter, *two Copies*
Mrs. Brereton, Ditto, *two Copies*
Rev. Mr. Bromley
Bryan Broughton, Efq. London
O. P. Brown, Efq.
Rev. Charles Prideaux Brune, Place, Cornwall, *two Copies*
Rev. Mr. Brutton, Sidmouth
Rev. Mr. Bryant, Chifelborough
James Bryant, Efq. Taunton
Mrs. Buck, Daddon
Rev. Charles Buckland, Axminfter
Rev. John Buckland
Mr. Buckley, *two Copies*
Rev. Dr. Buckner, Canon Refidentiary, Chichefter, *two Copies*
Rev. John Bull, Briftol
Dr. Buller, late Bifhop of Exeter, *ten Copies*
Sir Francis Buller, Bart. Lupton, *three Copies*
James Buller, Efq. Downs, *ten Copies*
Mr. Bullock, Bedford-Row, London, *two Copies*

Miss Ann Burd, Okehampton
William Burlton, Esq.
Mrs. P. Burlton, Bridgewater
Mrs. Burlton
Rev. T. Burrow, Inwardleigh
Rev. Dr. Burnaby, Archdeacon of Leicester
Thomas Burnaford, Esq. Tavistock
Mr. Burnard, Crewkerne
Rev. George Burrington, Chudleigh, *two Copies*
John Burton, Esq. Jacobstow, *eleven Copies*
Charles Burton, Esq.
Mrs. Bunney, Bath
Rev. J. Bussel
Rev. Thomas Butler, Child-Okeford, Dorset, *two Copies*
Mr. B. by the Rev. Mr. Luke
Mr. B.

C.

Countess Dowager of Chatham
Lord Clinton, *four Copies*
Lord Craig
Lady Camelford, *two Copies*
Lady Anne Carleton, *two Copies*
Lady Catherine Courtenay, *two Copies*
Lady Elizabeth Courtenay
Hon. Mrs. Colt, Scotland

Miss Colt, Scotland
Mrs. Cambridge
Mrs. Campbell, Karbric
Rev. James Camplin, Eastbury, Dorset, *two Copies*
Mrs. Camplin, Ditto, *two Copies*
Chapter of Canterbury, *twenty Copies*
Rev. Cornelius Cardew, Truro, Cornwall
Pole Carew, Esq.
Rev. J. W. Carew, Bickleigh, Devon
Rev. J. Carlyon, Truro, Cornwall
Thomas Carlyon, Esq. Tregrehane
Capt. Carlyon, Cornwall
John Carpenter, Esq. Tavyton, *two Copies*
Mrs. Carpenter, Ditto
John Carpenter, Esq. Launceston, *two Copies*
Rev. Dr. Carpenter, Ditto
Mr. Carpenter, Wincanton
John Carthew, Esq. Cornwall
Mr. Edmund Carthew, Liskeard
Mrs. Carthew, St. Austle
Mrs. Cartwright, Exeter, *two Copies*
Stephen Cave, Esq. Bristol, *ten Copies*
Rev. Mr. Carwithen, Newton St. Cyres
Mrs. Carwithen, Exeter
George Cary, Esq. Torr-Abbey, and Mrs. Cary, *four Copies*

B.

R. Chalmers, Esq.
Arthur Champernoun, Esq. Dartington, Devon, *four Copies*
Rev. John Charter, Holne, Ashburton
Thomas Chauntrell, Esq. London
Bishop of Chester, *two Copies*
J. P. Chichester, Esq. Arlington, Devon
R. B. Cholwich, Esq. Farringdon
Dean of Christ's Church
Peter Churchill, Esq. Dawlish
Rev. John Churchill, Rector of Eggesford, *ten Copies*
Rev. M. Churchill, Prebendary, Exeter, *two Copies*
Miss J. F. Churchill, Ditto
Mr. Churchill, Fellow of All Souls, Oxford
Rev. Mr. Churchward, Goodleigh
Rev. William Churchward, Goodleigh
Mrs. Sarah Churchward
R. H. Clarke, Esq. Bridwell, *two Copies*
Rev. Samuel Clarke, Belmont, Hants, *two Copies*
Mrs. Clarke, Ditto, *two Copies*
Rev. Thomas Clarke, Charmouth
Mrs. Clarke, of Mavisbank, Scotland
Mrs. Clavill, Smedmore, Dorset, *four Copies*
William Clay, Esq. London, *two Copies*
Rev. Benjamin Clay, East-Worlington
Mrs. Clay, Ditto
Mr. Cleather, Plymouth

Mr.

Mr. Cleave, Attorney, Crediton
John Cleveland, Esq. Tapley
Mrs. T. Clutterbuck, Truro, Cornwall
Mr. Andrew Cobley, East-Worlington, *two Copies*
Rev. T. Cockayne, Stapleton, Glocester
Rev. John Pyne Coffin, Portlege, Devon, *ten Copies*
Rev. Charles Pyne Coffin, East-Down, Devon, *two Copies*
Rev. W. H. Coham, Black Torrington
John Cole, Esq. Exeter, *five Copies*
James Colley, Esq. Little Torrington
B. F. Coleman, Esq. Bristol, *two Copies*
Mrs. Collins, Trevathen, *two Copies*
Miss Collins
George Collyns, Esq.
Mr. Collyns, Kenton
Mrs. Colmore, London
Rev. J. Comins, Rector of Rackenford
Rev. Dr. Conybeare
Rev. Dr. Cooke, Oxford, *ten Copies*
Mr. Richard Cook, West-Worlington
Mr. Coppleftone, Oxford
Rev. Charles Coppleftone, Rector of Radcliffe
Mr. P. Cornish, Surgeon, Exeter, *two Copies*
Dr. Cornwall, Dean of Canterbury, *ten Copies*
John Coryton, Esq. Cracadon, Cornwall, *ten Copies*
Rev. R. T. Cory

Rev.

Rev. J. Cory, Coſtiſloſt, Cornwall
Miſs Cory, Ditto
Miſs E. Cory, Ditto
Dr. Courtenay, Biſhop of Exeter, *two Copies*
Mrs. Couſe, Falmouth
Rev. Mr. Cox, Stockland
Mr. Coxe
General Craig
Robert Craig, Eſq. Advocate, Scotland
Rev. William Crakelt, London
Rev. Charles Crawley, Cliſt St. Mary, Devon
Mrs. Crofsley, Bath
Rev. Dr. Cruwys, Cruwys-Morchard
William Cubbin, Eſq. Liverpool
Dr. Cudlipp, Launceſton
John Culme, Eſq. Plymouth, *four Copies*
Rev. J. P. Cumming, New College, Oxon, *two Copies*
Rev. Mr. Curtis, All Souls, *ſix Copies*
Edward Curtis, Eſq. Oriel College, *two Copies*
Rev. Robert Cutcliffe, Seaton

D.

Earl of Darnley, *two Copies*
Earl of Dalkeith, *two Copies*
Lady Grace Douglas, Cavers, *two Copies*
Mrs. Douglas, Ditto

Lord

Lord Dunfinnan
Hon. Lord De Dunstanville, Tehiddy-Park Cornwall
Hon. Lady De Dunstanville
Lord Downe, Edinburgh, *six Copies*
Lady Downe, Ditto
Right Hon. Henry Dundas, *six Copies*
Hon. Mrs. Drummond, Bath
Mrs. Dale
Nathaniel Dalton, Esq. Shank's-House, Somerset
Mrs. Dalton
Miss Dalton, Pitcombe
Mrs. Damer, Bath
Thomas Daniell, Esq. Mincing-Lane, London, *twenty Copies*
Thomas Daniell, Esq. Bristol, *twenty Copies*
Samuel Daniell, Esq. Yeovil, Somerset, *two Copies*
Dr. Daniell, M. D. Crewkerne, *two Copies*
Ralph Allen Daniell, Esq. Truro
Mrs. Daniell, Ditto
Philip Dansey, Esq. *two Copies*
Mr. Dansey, Blandford
Mrs. J. Dansey, Ditto
Rev. A. Daubeny, Bristol, *two Copies*
Mr. Joseph Daubeney
Miss Daubuz, Cornwall
Sir John Davie, Bart. Creedy, Devon, *ten Copies*

Rev. Charles Davie, Buckland, *two Copies*
Mrs. C. Davies, *two Copies*
Mr. Davies
Ferdinand De Mierre, Efq. London, *two Copies*
Rev. Dr. De Salis
Mrs. Deacon, James-Street, Weftminfter
Rev. William Dean, Great Torrington
Nicholas Dennys, Efq. Afhley, Devon, *four Copies*
Alderman Dennis, Exeter
John Devayne, Efq. New-Street, Dorfet
John Devaynes, Efq. New Bond-Street
Rev. Richard Dibbin, Fontmill
Rev. Mr. Dicken, Witheridge, Devon
Rev. Edward Dickenfon, B. D. Rector of St. Mary Stafford
Rev. Henry Dillon, Lifkearde
Mr. Charles Dilly, *fix Copies*
Mifs Dixon, London
Rev. John Dobfon, Bath
Rev. Robert Doidge, *two Copies*
Sir William Dolben, Bart. M. P.
James Douglas, Efq. London, *four Copies*
Rev. Mr. W. Douglas, Salifbury
Mr. Dove, Wincanton
John Downman, Efq. London, *fix Copies*
Dr. Downman, Exeter, *four Copies*
Rev. Mr. Drake, Crewkerne

Rev.

Rev. Mr. Draper, Crewkerne
Thomas Rose Drewe, Esq. Wotton-House
William Drewe, Esq. Spring-Gardens
Archibald Drummond, M. D. Ridgeway, Glocester, *four Copies*
Andrew Drummond, Esq. Ditto, *four Copies*
Mrs. Drummond
Robert Dundas, Esq. *four Copies*
Mrs. Christian Dundas, Melville-Castle, Scotland, *two Copies*
Mrs. Mary Knight Damer, Bridgewater
Mr. B. Dunsterville, Surgeon, Plymouth
Mr. John Dunsterville, Exeter College, Oxon
S. Dupuy, Esq. Taunton, *two Copies*
Miss Dupuy, Ditto

E.

Right Hon. Countess Dowager Ely, Bath
Right Hon. Lord and Lady Eliot, *six Copies*
Hon. John Eliot, Port Eliot
Miss Eliot, Ditto
Lord Eskgrove, Edinburgh
Mr. Eales, Plymouth
Miss Eastcott
Rev. H. R. Edwards
Rev. W. E. Edwards, Redland, *two Copies*

Rev. J. Edwards, Rector of Berry Pomeroy
Mr. Edwards, London, *two Copies*
Samuel Edwards, Efq. Cotham, Gloucester
William Egerton, Efq.
Rev. Charles Egerton, Thorncombe
William Elford, Efq. M. P. Bickham
Jonathan Elford, Efq. Plymouth-Dock
Rev. William Ellicombe, Alphington
Rev. H. Ellicombe
Mr. Elliker
Mr. Ellis, Wincanton
Mifs Ellis, Exeter, *two Copies*
John Elmefley, Efq. Fellow of Oriel College, *ten Copies*
Rev. William Elfton, Weft-Down
Robert Cary Elwes, Efq.
Rev. Mr. Eton, Archdeacon of Middlefex
Rev. Mr. Evans, Eton
Mrs. Evans, Bath
Rev. Dr. Eveleigh, Provoft of Eton, *two Copies*
Rector of Exeter College, Oxon

F.

Earl Fortefcue, *ten Copies*
Lady Fortefcue, *ten Copies*
Hon. Capt. Fortefcue, *ten Copies*
Thomas Falconer, Efq. Bath

Mrs.

Mrs. Faneuil, Stonehouse
John Fanshawe, Esq. Wimpole-Street
Mrs. Fanshawe, Ditto
Miss Fanshawe, Ditto
Miss C. Fanshawe, Ditto
Rev. R. Farmer
Mrs. Fazerkerly, *six Copies*
Joseph Feltham, Esq. Hinton, Somersetshire
Rev. Mr. Fewtrell, Crewkerne
Professor Finlayson
Rev. Peter Fisher, Little Torrington
Miss Fisher
Mrs. Foley, Bath
Rev. John Follett, Tiverton
Mr. Foote, Southmolton
A. Forbes, Esq. of Culloden
Rev. Mr Forrester, Thurston, Leicester
Inglet Fortescue, Esq.
Mrs. Fortescue, Dawlish, *two Copies*
Miss M. Fortescue, *two Copies*
Rev. Mr. Foss, Arlington
Rev. Dr. Foster, Eton, *two Copies*
Dr. Fothergill, Bath
Rev. Peter Fowkes, *two Copies*
Rev. Thomas Fownes, Kittery, *two Copies*
Rev. F. Foxcroft, Winterbourn, *two Copies*

Mrs. Fraine, Bath
A Friend, *two Copies*, by Mrs. Vivian, Pencarlinick
Ditto, *two Copies*, by Ditto
Mr. William Fripp, Briftol
Mrs. Froome, Salifbury, *two Copies*
Rev. Robert Hurrell Froude, Totnefs, *four Copies*
Rev. James Furneaux, Plymouth
Rev. Peter Wellington Furfe, Halfdon
Philip Furze, Efq. Briftol

G.

Earl of Grofvenor, *two Copies*
Hon. Mifs Gray, Edinburgh
Lady Glanville
Lord Grenville, *ten Copies*
Lord Gwydir, *two Copies*
Henry Gally, Efq. *two Copies*
Rev. J. Gandy, Rector of Old Church, Plymouth, and Prebendary of Exeter Cathedral, *ten Copies*
John Gape, Efq. Bath, *two Copies*
Mr. Joel Gardener, Briftol, *two Copies*
Mrs. Joel Gardener, Ditto, *two Copies*
Rev. Mr. Garnett, Prebendary of Winchefter
Mrs. Garnier
Dr. Gafking, Plymouth
Mr. Gater, Exeter, *two Copies*

Rev.

Rev. Nicholas Gay, Vicar, Up-Ottery
Miſs Gay, Cloiſter-Hall
Miſs Gennys, Stonehouſe, Plymouth, *two Copies*
A Gentleman, *ten Copies*, by the Rev. Mr. Karſlake
A Gentleman, Eton, *four Copies*
A Gentleman, *two Copies*
A Gentleman, by Mrs. Prideaux
A Gentleman, by the Rev. J. Churchill
Rev. John Gibbons, Bath
Rev. Mr. Gibbons, Windſor
Vicary Gibbs, Eſq. London, *ten Copies*
Miſs Gibbs, Heywood-Houſe, Wilts, *ten Copies*
Mr. Gidley, Crewkerne
Walter Rawleigh Gilbert, Eſq. Priory-Houſe, *four Copies*
Mrs. W. R. Gilbert, Ditto, *four Copies*
Rev. Edmond Gilbert
Miſs Catherine Gilbert
Rev. William Gillett, Glouceſter
Dr. Girod, Exeter
F. Glanville, Eſq. Catch-French
Mrs. Glanville, Ditto
Dr. Glaſs, Greenford
Rev. George Glaſs, Ditto
Rev. Thomas Glubb, Exeter College, Oxon
John Warren Glubb, Eſq. Torrington
Rev. Peter Glubb, Rector of Langtree

Mrs. Glynn, Crefcent, Bath
Rev. Mr. Goodall, Eton
Robert Goodden, Efq. Compton, Dorfet, *two Copies*
Wyndham Goodden, Efq. Clifton
Mifs Goodden, Bath
Mrs. Goodenough, Wigmore-Street, London, *two Copies*
Mrs. Goodford, Yeovil, Somerfet, *two Copies*
Rev. Mr. Gordon, Chaplain of Exeter Cathedral, *ten Copies*
Mrs. Gordon, Hartland
Rev. Charles Gore, Henbury, Gloucefter, *two Copies*
Mrs. Gore, Dunfcombe
George Gould, Efq. Upway, Dorfet
Rev. Robert Gould, Motherton, Devon
Edmund Granger, Efq. Exeter, *two Copies*
Mr. William Gravener, Briftol
Mrs. Graves, Bath
Thomas Greening, Efq. Ditto, *two Copies*
Mrs. W. Gregor
Pafcoe Grenfill, Efq. Marazion, *two Copies*
William Grey, Efq. Crewkerne
Mrs. Grills, Helftone, *two Copies*
Mifs Grills, Ditto
Rev. R. P. Grills, Ditto
Rev. Thomas Grove, Meer, Wilts
Rev. Mr. Guirdner, Eton

Nathaniel

Nathaniel Gundry, Efq. *two Copies*
Mrs. Gundry, *two Copies*
Mrs. M. Gundry, Richmond, *two Copies*
Thomas Gundry, Efq. Dewlifh, Dorfet, *two Copies*
Rev. Dr. Gunning, *two Copies*
Mrs. Gunning
John Gunfton, Efq. Bath
Mrs. Gwatkin, Ditto
Capt. Gwennapp, Bideford

H.

Earl of Hardwicke, *twenty Copies*
Earl of Hadington, *four Copies*
Lady Harewood, *four Copies*
Lady Hamilton
Lady Hope
Hon. Mrs. Hood
Lord Hawkefbury, *two Copies*
Lord Vifcount Hood, *two Copies*
Hon. Henry Hood
Rev. William Hains, Vicar of Overton, *two Copies*
Mrs. Hale, Ingfdon, *four Copies*
Dr. Hall, Bodmin
John Hallett, Efq. Mifterton, Somerfet
Rev. Richard Hallett, Stedcombe
Rev. Richard Hammett, Hartland

Sir Alexander Hamilton, Retreat, Devon
—— Hamilton, Efq. Curzon-Street, May-Fair
Mr. Robert Hamlyn, Bideford
Mrs. Hamlyn, Pafcoe
Rev. Mr. W. Hannington
R. Harding, Efq. *two Copies*
Rev. Dr. Hardwicke, Sodbury, Gloucefter, *two Copies*
George Hardwicke, M. D. Ditto, *two Copies*
Mrs. Hare, Plymouth
Edward Harford, Efq. Briftol, *four Copies*
Jofeph Harford, Efq. Ditto, *four Copies*
John Scandret Harford, Efq. Ditto
Samuel Lloyd Harford, Efq. Ditto, *four Copies*
Charles Jofeph Harford, Efq. Ditto, *four Copies*
James Butler Harris, Efq. Powy's-Place, London
Mrs. Harris, Bath
Mifs Harris, Hayne, Cornwall
Mrs. Harris, Truro
Mrs. Harris, Rofewarne
Mr. Harrifon, *four Copies*
Mifs Harrifon, Bath
C. B. Hart, Efq. Sidborough
Mr. Harpur, Surgeon, Truro
Mifs Harpur, Redruth
William Hawker, Efq. Poundisford, Somerfet
Mifs Hawker, Ditto

Mrs.

(xxvii)

Mrs. Hawker, Long-Parish, Eton, *two Copies*
Mrs. Hawkins, Kelston-House, Bath
Stephen Hawtrey, Esq.
Mrs. L. Hawtrey, Eton
Mrs. F. Hawtrey, Ditto
James Hay, Esq. Drumellier, Scotland
Mrs. Hay, Ditto
Mrs. Hay
Mr. Haydon, Crewkerne
John Hayes, Esq.
Rev. George Hayter, Isle of Wight, *two Copies*
Mrs. Hearle, Helligan
Rev. Dr. George Heath, Eton, *ten Copies*
Mrs. Heath, Ditto
Rev. Dr. Heath, Ditto
Rev. Canon Heberden, Exeter, *ten Copies*
Dr. Heberden, Pall-Mall, *two Copies*
Dr. William Heberden, Down-Street, Berkly-Sqnare, *two Copies*
G. Heinzalman, Esq. Heavitree, Devon
William Helyar, Esq. Coker, Somerset, *twenty Copies*
Mrs. Helyar, Ditto, *ten Copies*
Edward Helyar, Esq. Ditto, *two Copies*
Weston Helyar, Esq. Newton Ferrers, Cornwall, *two Copies*
Miss Helyars, Bath, *ten Copies*

Mrs. Herring, Great Torrington
Rev. Dr. Hey, Canon, Chriſt-Church, *four Copies*
Mrs. Heyes, Bath
John Heywood, Eſq. Inner-Temple, *two Copies*
Mr. William Hicks, Exeter
Mr. E. Hicker, Richmond
Mr. John Hiern, Torrington
Rev. Mr. Hiern, Stoke, Devon
James Hill, Eſq. *two Copies*
Mrs. Hill
Richard Hill, Eſq. Plymouth-Lodge, Cardiff
Thomas Hill, Eſq. Briſtol
Rev. Mr. Hill, Tawſtock, Devon
John Hilton, Eſq. *two Copies*
Rev. Mr. Hinde, Eton
R. Hippeſley, Eſq.
Rev. H. Hippeſley
Henry Hoare, Eſq. Fleet-Street
Mrs. Hoare, Ditto
Mr. C. Hoare, Dawliſh
Miſs Hodſon
Mrs. Holdſworth, Dartmouth, *ten Copies*
Rev. Thomas Hole, Ham, Devon
Rev. H. A. Hole, Rector of Chumleigh
Rev. Joſhua Hole, Vicar of Burrington
Rev. William Holland, Bath, *two Copies*

Mrs.

Mrs. Holland, Portsmouth
Mrs. Holman, Bath
John Holmes, Esq.
Mr. William Holmes, Exeter
Mrs. Ann Holwell, Ditto, *two Copies*
Rev. John Honey, Liskearde
Rev. John Honywood, Bath
Mr. John Hosegood, West-Worlington, Devon
Thomas Hoskins, Esq. Haslebury, Somerset, *two Copies*
William Hoskins, Esq. Perrot-House, *two Copies*
Rev. David Horndon, *two Copies*
Rev. Thomas Horndon, Bath
Rev. Canon Howell, Exeter, *ten Copies*
David Howell, Esq. *four Copies*
Mrs. Howell, Bath, *two Copies*
Miss Howell, Ditto
Mrs. Hudson, Exeter
Henry Hughes, Esq.
William Hunt, Esq.
Rev. William Hunt, Plymouth
Mrs. Hurrel, and Miss Davie, *two Copies*

I.

Hon. Mrs. Irby
Sir James Norcliffe Innes, Bart. Innes-House
Lieutenant-Colonel Incledon, First Regiment

R.

R. N. Incledon, Efq. Pilton, Devon
Joſhua Ironmonger, Efq.
Mrs. Ironmonger
Mrs. Irwin, London
Miſs Iſaac, *two Copies*
Mr. D'Iſraelli, London
E. I.
William Jackſon, Efq. Exeter, *ten Copies*
William Jackſon, Efq. Junr. Cowley, *twenty Copies*
Thomas Jackſon, Efq. Secretary of Legation, at Turin, *ten Copies*
F. J. Jackſon, Efq. *two Copies*
William Bickford Jackſon, Efq. Bideford
William Adair Jackſon, Efq. South-Sea-Houſe
Rev. Dr. Jackſon
Rev. J. Jago, Vicar of Milton Abbott
Miſs Jago, Mevagiſſey
Jarvoiſe Clerk Jarvoiſe, Efq. Belmont, Hants, *two Copies*
Thomas Clerk Jarvoiſe, Efq. Ditto, *two Copies*
Rev. J. R. I'Ans
Mrs. Jeffery, Bath, *four Copies*
Mrs. Jenny, Truro
Miſs Jenny, Ditto
Mr. Jeſſe
Richard Johns, Efq. Helſtone
Mrs. Johns

William Johnson, Efq. London
William Johnson, Efq. King's College, Cambridge
Thomas Jones, Efq. Stapleton, Gloucefter, *four Copies*
Rev. Dr. Jones, Archdeacon of Hereford, *two Copies*
Rev. Thomas Jones, Hill-Houfe, *two Copies*
Rev. Richard Jones, Charfield
Mr. William Jones, No. 141, Bond-Street, London
Mr. Jones, Eton
Mrs. Jones, Blandford
Mrs. Joy

K.

Rev. Mr. Karflake, Bifhop's Nympton, *two Copies*
Mr. William Karflake
Mr. Keate
Rev. Mr. Keats, King's Nympton
Mr. James Kemp, Truro
Rev. Nicholas Kendal, Pelyn
Rev. Mr. Kerrick
Thomas Kevill, Efq. Trevenfan, *two Copies*
Mr. Mervin King, Exeter
Richard Kingdon, Efq. Barum
Mr. Kipling
Charles Kitfon, Efq. *ten Copies*
Rev. Walter Kitfon, Exeter, *two Copies*
Rev. E. A. Kitfon, Ditto, *two Copies*

Rev.

Rev. Thomas Kitson, Shiphay
Rev. William Kitson, Torquay
Mrs. Knapton, Dorset

L.

Lady Langham, Cavendish-Square, London, *two Copies*
Madam Lambert, Wales
Thomas Lane, Esq. Coffleet, *ten Copies*
A Lady, by Ditto, *twenty Copies*
A Lady unknown, to be sent to Mrs. Welsford, Totnes, *twelve Copies*
A Lady unknown, to be sent to Ditto, *ten Copies*
A Lady unknown, to be sent to Ditto, *six Copies*
A Lady, *four Copies*
A Lady
A Lady, Bath
A Lady
Rev. J. Lamb, Vicar of Banbury, Oxford
Rev. John Land, Thruiscik, *two Copies*
Miss Land, Dartmouth
Mr. Philip Lane, Morchard-Bishop
Rev. Dr. Langford, Eton
Rev. Mr. E. Langford, Ditto
Rev. Dr. Law, Archdeacon of Rochester, *two Copies*
Mrs. Le Fevre, Bedford-Square, London, *two Copies*
George Leach, Esq. Plymouth

Thomas Leare, Esq. Sandwell, Devon
Mr. Lee, Ilfracombe
Mrs. Lee, Bath
Rev. Mr. Leeves, Ditto
Mr. Leicester, Eton
Rev. George Leigh, Ellicombe, Somerset, *two Copies*
Rev. Charles Lethbridge, St. Stephen's, Cornwall
Mr. Christopher Lethbridge, Launceston
Nathaniel William Lewis, Esq. Bath
Mrs. Lewis, *two Copies*
Mrs. Lewis
John Ley, Esq. Trehill, *two Copies*
Henry Ley, Esq. Exeter, *two Copies*
Mrs. Ley, Ashprington
Rev. Jacob Ley, Rector of Ditto
Rev. Mr. Ley, Shobrooke
Mr. George Ley, Cockington
Mrs. Lillington, Bath
Rev. Mr. Linch, Archdeacon of Canterbury, *twenty Copies*
Sir Henry Lippencott, Bart. Stike, Gloucester, *two Copies*
Rev. Mr. Loudon, *two Copies*
Matthew Louis, Esq. Calcutta, Bengal, *fifty Copies*
Miss Louis, Edinburgh, *ten Copies*
Capt. Louis, of the Navy, *ten Copies*

Mr. Louis, Exeter
Miſs Elizabeth Louis, Ditto, *four Copies*
Miſs F. E. Louis, Ditto, *four Copies*
Miſs S. Louis
Robert Harvey Lovell, Eſq. Coal-Park, *four Copies*
Dr. Lovell, Briſtol
Rev. T. M. Lovering, Pinhoe
Thomas Lowfield, Eſq. Bath, *two Copies*
Rev. Mr. Luce, Plymouth
Abraham Ludlow, M. D. Briſtol, *ten Copies*
Abraham Ludlow, Junr. Eſq. Royal North Britiſh Dragoons, *ten Copies*
Rev. Mr. Luke, Exeter, *two Copies*
John Fownes Luttrell, Eſq. Dunſter Caſtle
Francis Fownes Luttrell, Eſq. *two Copies*
Rev. Mr. Luxmoore, Prebendary of Canterbury, *ten Copies*
Henry Luxmoore, Eſq. Okehampton
Mr. T. B. Luxmoore, Ditto
Mrs. Charles Luxmoore, Ditto
Rev. Coryndon Luxmoore, Brideſtow
Rev. John Luxton
Rev. Richard Lyne, St. Ives, Cornwall
Rev. Philip Lyne, L. L. D. Vicar of Mevagiſſey
Dr. Lyſons, Bath, *two Copies*
A. L. Ditto

Earl

M.

Earl of Moray, *ten Copies*
Dowager Lady Molefworth, Cornwall, *four Copies*
Lord Montague, *two Copies*
Hon. Mr. Marfham
Hon. Mrs. Marfham, *two Copies*
Sir William Molefworth, Bart. Pencarrow, Cornwall
Lady Molefworth, Ditto
John Mackrafs, Efq.
John Mallet, Efq. Speccott
Mifs Ann Mallet, Taunton
Mrs. Mander, Truro
Mrs. John Manley
Richard Manfel, Efq. Bath
Mifs March, Briftol, *two Copies*
Rev. R. J. Marker, Uffculme
Major-General Marfh, Bolton-Row
Rev. George Marfh, Critchel, Devon
Rev. Edward Marfhall, Breage, Cornwall
William Mafters, Efq.
Rev. William Mafters, Vicar of Sparfhold, Hants
James Martin, Efq. Temple, *two Copies*
Mifs Martin, Seaborough
Mrs. Martyn, Bath, *two Copies*
Rev. J. Maule, Park-Row, Greenwich

Rev. James May, Cheldon
John Mayo, Esq. Bath
Mrs. Meddon
Mrs. Medlycott, Ven-House, Dorset
Rev. Mr. Meekins, Oxford
Richard Melluish, Esq. Witheridge, *two Copies*
J. Merry, Esq. London, *two Copies*
Warden of Merton College, Oxon, *two Copies*
John Merrivale, Esq. Devon, *four Copies*
Mr. Messer, Surgeon
Joseph Metford, Esq. *two Copies*
Miss Michell, Redruth
Miss Middletons, Hill-Street, Berkley-Square, *two Copies*
John Milford, Esq. Exeter, *two Copies*
Richard Milford, Esq. Bath
William Miles, Esq. Clifton, *four Copies*
Rev. William Millars, Fellow of St. John's College, Cambridge
Miss Millar, Queen's-Street, May-Fair, London
Miss Milles, Ditto
Langford Millington, Esq. London
George Mills, Esq.
Mrs. Mills
Rev. William Forord Mitchell, Rector of Throwleigh
Mrs. Mitchell, Dewlish, Dorset
Abraham Moore, Esq. Temple, *two Copies*

Mrs. Moore, Grampound
Rev. Archdeacon Moore, Exeter, *ten Copies*
Rev. William Moore, Senr. Southtawton, *two Copies*
Rev. William Moore
Rev. Thomas Moore, Bifhop's Tawton
Rev. Edward Moore, Oxford
Rev. Mr. Montgomery, Vicar of Stewkly, *two Copies*
Mr. R. Montgomery
Rev. H. Morgan, Canon, Hereford
General Morrifon, No. 62, Upper Seymour-Street
Mrs. E. Morrifon, Bideford
Rev. H. Morrifon, Yeovale
Rev. T. Morrifon
P. Morfhead, Efq. Widey, *two Copies*
Mrs. Mortimer
Mifs Moyle, Park-Row, Greenwich
Rev. Mr. Mules, Ilminfter
Mrs. Munday, Budleigh-Salterton
Mr. Murray

N.

His Grace the Duke of Northumberland, *four Copies*
Lady Napier, Bath, *two Copies*
Sir Stafford Henry Northcote, *five Copies*
Mrs. T. Nankivel
Richard Nelmes, Efq. Briftol, *two Copies*

Rev. Mr. New
—— Newcombe, Efq. Teignmouth, *two Copies*
John Nicholas, Efq. Mincing-Lane
Mrs. Nicholls, Terriff, Cornwall, *two Copies*
Dr. Nowell, Principal of St. Mary's-Hall, Oxford, *two Copies*
Rev. Chancellor Nutcombe, Exon, *two Copies*
George Nutcombe, Efq. *two Copies*
Mifs Nutcombe

O.

Rev. Henry Oglander, Fairy-Hill, Ifle of Wight
Rev. Newton Ogle, D. D. Dean of Winchefter
Mifs Oke
Mr. Parry Okeden
Paul Orchard, Efq. Hartland-Abbey, *ten Copies*
Mrs. Ouchterloney, Topfham
Mrs. Ourry
Mr. Owen, London

P

Right Hon. Earl Paulet, *two Copies*
Lady Paulet, Lyme, Dorfet
Lord and Lady Portfmouth, *ten Copies*
Lady Porchefter, Pixton Houfe, *two Copies*

Lady

Lady Pellew, Flushing
The Lord President, Edinburgh
Hon. Philip Percy, *four Copies*
Hon. Mrs. Paterson
Francis Page, Esq.
Lawrence Palk, Esq. Haldon-House, *fifteen Copies*
Walter Palk, Esq. Marley House
Rev. Lawrence Panting, *two Copies*
Thomas Parlby, Esq. Stone Hall, *two Copies*
John Partridge, Esq. Great Torrington
John Patch, Esq. London
George Paterson, Esq. Castle Huntley, Scotland
Mrs. Patterson, Ditto, *two Copies*
William Payne, Esq. Bristol, *two Copies*
Mrs. Pellew, Falmouth
Rev. Robert Penny, D. D. Rector of Cromhall, and Chaplain to his Grace the Duke of Beaufort, *two Copies*
Rev. John Penrose, Carwarthenick, Cornwall
Mrs. M. Penrose, Ditto
Mrs. Charles Penrose, Breage, Ditto
Rev. Thomas Penwarne, Cornwall
Mr. Perfect, Wincanton
Peter Perring, Esq. *four Copies*
Rev. John Perring, by Mr. F. Barnes
Rev. John Perry, Herts, *two Copies*

Mrs. Perry, Herts, *two Copies*
Mrs. Peppin, Dulverton, Somerset
Henry Peters, Esq. No. 50, Park-street
Mrs. Peters, Ditto
Sir John Philips, Newport House, Cornwall, *two Copies*
Rev. J. Phillips, Membury
Miss Phillips, Ditto
Mrs. Phillips, Topsham
Mr. Pickford, Oriel College, Oxford, *two Copies*
Miss Mary Pierce, Exeter
Mrs. Pigott, Dartmouth
Arthur Pigott, Esq. Powys Place
Miss F. D. Pindar, Trelissick, Cornwall
Mrs. Pinny, Upper Charlotte-street
John Platel, Esq. London
Mrs. Pleydell, Blandford, *forty Copies*
Miss Pleydell, Ditto, *two Copies*
Miss Mary Pleydell, Ditto, *two Copies*
Mrs. Mary Pleydell, Twickenham, *two Copies*
Mrs. Cornelia Pleydell, Ditto, *two Copies*
Major Pleydell, Dorset, *two Copies*
Edmund Morton Pleydell, Esq. Whatcombe, Ditto, *four Copies*
Rev. Mr. Plumptree, Pref. Worcester
Sir John De la Pole, Shute House
Miss Polwhele, Truro

Mrs. Poole, Bath
Rev. Mr. Poole, Oriel, *two Copies*
Rev. Henry Pooley, Truro
Mr. Joseph Porter, London
Rev. Mr. Poulter, Prebendary, Winchester
Mrs. Poor, Salisbury
Richard Newdicote Poynty, Esq. Tormartin, Gloucester
Rev. Mr. Price, Merriott, Somerset, *two Copies*
Mr. Samuel Price, East Worlington
Rev. John Price, Keeper of the Bodleian Lib. Oxford
Rev. Richard Price, Lamerton
Mrs. Prideaux, Bath, *four Copies*
A Gentleman, by Mrs. Prideaux
Mr. Prowse, Exeter
Arthur Puckey, Esq. Liskeard, *two Copies*
Mrs. Puckey, Ditto
Mrs. Putt, Bridestow
Rev. Thomas Putt, Corpus College, Oxford, *two Copies*
Rev. Edward Pyne, East Down, Devon
Mr. William Pyne, Bristol

Q

Lady Francis Quin
Mrs. Quenoualt, Taunton
Mrs. Quicke, Bath, *two Copies*

R.

Lord Rolle, Stevenftone, *ten Copies*
Hon. Lord Romney
Lady Rofs, Bath
Hon. Mr. Juftice Rook
Richard Coppleftone Radcliffe, Stoke
Rev. John Radford, Lapford
Mifs Rae, Edinburgh
Mrs. Rambouillet, Bath
Rev. Dr. Randolph, Ditto, *two Copies*
Rev. Dr. Randolph, Regius Profeffor of Divinity, Oxford
P. Rafhleigh, Efq. Menabilly, Cornwall
Charles Rafhleigh, Efq. St. Auftle
Mifs Redwood, Bath
Richard Reed, Efq. Trevalas, Cornwall
Dr. Remmet, Plymouth, *two Copies*
Mr. Rendall, Wincanton
Mrs. Reynolds, Penair, Truro, *two Copies*
Rev. George Rhodes, Colyton, Devon
Philip Richards, Efq. Penryn
Rev. John Richards
Mrs. Richards, Cambourne
Rev. William Richards, Stour Provoft, Dorfet
Mr. T. Ridout, Scaborough
Mr. John Ridout, Ditto, Somerfet

(xliii)

William Roberts, Efq. Exeter, *four Copies*
Mifs Roberts, Penryn, Cornwall
Rev. Mr. Roberts
Mr. Thomas Roberts, Briftol
Mifs Robinfon, Helfton
Mr. Robinfon
Lieut.-Colonel Rodd, Trebartha, Cornwall, *fix Copies*
Mrs. H. Rodd
R. Rofenhagen, Efq. Royal Hofpital, Greenwich, *fix Copies*
Rev. J. Rowe, Alfcott, Devon
James Rowe, Efq. Ditto, *two Copies*
Mifs D. M. Rowe
Mrs. P. Rowe, London
Mifs Rowe, Tiverton, *two Copies*
Rev. John Ruffel
E. R.

S.

Countefs of Strafford
Lady Anne Stuart, Scotland, *ten Copies*
Lady Sommers
Hon. Arch. Stuart, Blandford, *four Copies*
The Bifhop of Salifbury
Rev. Mr. Salmon, Crewkerne

Rev. Thomas Saltren, Petticombe
Mrs. Sambell, Mevagiffey
Capt Samber, Navy
Robert Dundas Sanders, Efq.
Mifs Sandfords, Bath
Mrs. Sandford, Walford, Somerfetfhire
Mrs. Sandford, Ninehead
J. Satterthwayte, Efq. London
Mrs. Sawle, Penryn, Cornwall, *two Copies*
Mifs Bridget Sawle, Exeter, *four Copies*
Mrs. Sayre, Bath, *two Copies*
Mrs. Sayre, *two Copies*
Sir William Scott
J. B. Sealy, D. D. F. R. S. Stefted, Effex
Mifs Sealey, Bridgewater
Mrs. Segre
Mrs. J. Senhoufe, Mincing-Lane, London
Mrs. Sheere, Bideford
Rev. George Sherrard
Mrs. Sherrard
John Jeffery Short, Efq. Exeter, *ten Copies*
Mrs. Shute, Stapleton, Gloucefterfhire, *two Copies*
Rev. Mr. Shute, Ditto, *two Copies*
Thomas Shute, Efq. Wotton
Mr. Sigmond, Bath, *two Copies*
Mrs. Sillifant

Mifs Sinclair
Rev. Mr. Sirvage, Eton, *four Copies*
Sir John Skinner, *two Copies*
Mrs. Skinner, Clofe, Exeter, *two Copies*
Rev. Dr. John Skinner
Rev. Richard Slade, Torrington
Rev. Richard Sleeman
Charles Smith, Efq. Queen Anne's-ftreet, Weftminfter, *two Copies*
Mr. H. Smyth, Royal Hofpital, Greenwich
Rev. Stafford Smyth, Prior Park, Bath
Charles Smyth, Efq.
Rev. William Smyth, Bideford, *four Copies*
Rev. William Southmead, Rector of Gidley
Mr. Ifaac Spaiks, Ditto
John Span, Efq. Briftol, *two Copies*
T. Sparkes, Efq. Ditto
Mr. Speare, No. 5, Leadenhall-ftreet, *two Copies*
Mr. George Spencer, Eaft Worlington
Thomas Splatt, Efq. Brixton, *two Copies*
Rev. Chriftopher Spry
Rev. Mr. Spurway, Pilton, Devon
Rev. William Spurway, Barnftaple
Mrs. St. Aubyn, Bath
Rev. Mr. Stabback
Mrs. Stackhoufe, Pendaroes

Mr. Joseph Staines, Ironmonger
Mrs. Stapleton, Burton Pynsent, Somerset
Miss Staunton, New Norfolk-street
Rev. W. M. Stawell, Southmolton
Rev. Charles Steer, Axminster
Miss Sterling, Scotland
Miss Sterling, Keir, Ditto
Rev. Dr. Stevens
Rev. Mr. Stevenson, Eton
James Still, Esq. Knoyle, Wilts, *two Copies*
Rev. John Still, Ditto, *two Copies*
Mrs. Still, Ditto
Miss Stona
Thomas Strong, Esq. Lympstone, *two Copies*
Andrew Strahan, Esq. London
Rev. Dr. Sturges, Chanc. Dioc. Winton, *ten Copies*
Mrs. Sumbell
Mr. William Sunter, Ashburton
Mr. Joseph Sunter, Ditto
—— Sutton, Esq. New Park, Wilts, *two Copies*
Mrs. Sutton, Ditto, *two Copies*
Mr. William Swanson
Rev. Thomas Sweet
Mrs. Sweet, Kentisbury
Mrs. Symons
Miss Symons

Mr.

Mr. William Symons, Plymouth
Mr. James Renal Syms

T.

Lady Talbot
Right Hon. Lady Charlotte Townſhend
Lady Tynte, Haſwel, Somerſet, *two Copies*
Preſident of Trinity College, Oxon
Henry Tahourdin, Eſq. London, *two Copies*
Rev. Robert Tarrant, Exeter, *two Copies*
Mr. Tatnell, Greenwich
Mrs. Mary Tatnell, Ditto
Dr. Taunton, Bath
Mrs. Taunton, Truro
Mrs. Pearce Taylor, Ogwill, *two Copies*
Thomas Taylor, Eſq. Denbury, *two Copies*
Rev. Mr. Taylor, Clifton, *two Copies*
Rev. Edward Taylor, Bifrous, Kent, *two Copies*
D. Taylor, Eſq. Wotton Underedge
Rev. J. Templar, Lindridge, *four Copies*
Rev. John Templeman, Sopen, Somerſet
Rev. Thomas Thelwall, M. A.
Mrs. Theobald
John Thomas, Eſq.
Rev. G. A. Thomas, Maize Hill, Greenwich
Mr. Thorne, Wincanton

Rev.

Rev. F. Thurlston, Leicestershire
Mr. Tickle, Bath
Mrs. A. Tippetts, Ditto
Mr. Tippett, Falmouth
Mrs. Todd, Ditto
Rev. T. Todd
Rev. M. Tomkins
Rev. Mr. Tomkins, R. South Perrot, *two Copies*
Rev. William Toms, Southmolton
Mr. Peter Tonkin
Torrington Book Club
Rev. Mr. Totten, Oriel College, Oxon
Mrs. Towers, Bath
Mr. Towle
Francis Towne, Esq. *two Copies*
Miss Townley
Mr. John Townshend, Bristol
Rev. John Trefusis, South Hill
Arthur Tremayne, Esq. Sydenham, *eleven Copies*
Rev. H. H. Tremayne, Helligan
Rev. Dr. Trenchard, Lytchet
Mrs. Trelawney, Lostwithiel
Mrs. Trevenen, Sen.
John Trevenen, Esq. Helston
Mrs. Trevenen, Ditto
Rev. Tho. Trevenen, Cardinham, Cornwall, *two Copies*

Mr.

Mr. Trevoſſa, Falmouth
Meſſrs. Trewman and Son, *two Copies*
Rev. R. Tripp, Rewe
Allar Tucker, Eſq. Bideford
Miſs Tucker, Uffculme
Miſs S. Tucker, Ditto
Rev. Peter Tucker, Morchard
Rev. G. Tucker, L. L. D. Axminſter
Henry Tuckfield, Eſq. *two Copies*
Mrs. Tuckfield, *two Copies*
Miſs Tudor
Mr. Thomas Turner, Attorney, Exeter
Mr. Turner, Redland
Thomas Tyndall, Eſq. Briſtol, *two Copies*
Rev. W. R. Tyſon
William Twopenny, Eſq.
Mr. Edward Twopenny
Rev. Richard Twopenny, Oriel College, *ten Copies*

U. and V.

Mrs. Udney
Unknown, *two Copies*
Richard Vaughan, Eſq. Briſtol, *two Copies*
Rev. Mr. Veyſey, *ten Copies*
Rev. T. Stonehouſe Vigor, Clifton, *two Copies*
Admiral Vincent, *ſixty Copies*
Thomas Vincent, Eſq. Weſt Stour

Mr. Viner, Furnivals Inn
John Vivian, Efq. Bedford-fquare, *two Copies*
Mrs. Vivian, *two Copies*
J. Vivian, Jun. Efq. Temple, London, *two Copies*
Rev. H. Vivian
Mrs. Vivian, Pencarlinick, *ten Copies*
Rev. J. Vivian, Ditto, *five Copies*
Mifs Vivian
Matthew Vivian, Efq. Rofewarne
Mrs. M. Vivian
Rev. Henry Vivian
Mrs. John Vivian, Truro
Rev. Dr. Vyner, *two Copies*
Major-General Vyfe
Thomas Vyvyan, Efq.

W.

Lady Willoughby, of Erefby, *two Copies*
Lady Dowager Wrey, Bath, *two Copies*
Warden of Wadham College, Oxford, *two Copies*
Mr. Daniel Wait
Rev. Robert Walker, Cornwall
Mrs. Walker, Loftwithiel
Thomas Walker, Efq. London, *ten Copies*
Mifs Mary Walker
Thomas Walker, Efq. Ridland, *ten Copies*

Mrs.

Mrs. Wallis, Bodmin
Rev. William Walter
Joseph Ward, Esq. Bath
John Warren, Esq. Oriel College, Oxford, *two Copies*
Miss Warren, *four Copies*
Mrs. Wathen, Bath
Mr. Watson, Bideford
James Watson, Esq.
Sir Charles Watson
Mrs. Watson
Mr. Edward Watts, Crewkerne
Mr. Wause
Mrs. Wayte, Bath
John Fisher Weare, Esq. *four Copies*
Mrs. Webb, Truro
Mrs. Webb, Bath
Nathaniel Webb, Esq. Round Hill, Somerset
Mrs. Webb, Ditto
W. Webber, Esq. Vanbrugh-House, Kent, *two Copies*
Rev. Samuel Wells, Portlemouth
Mrs. Welsford, Totnes, *two Copies*
Mrs. John Welsford, London, *two Copies*
Mrs. West, Upper Charlotte-street
Mr. Westbrough, Bristol
Miss F. Weston, Exeter
Rev. S. Weston, Prebendary, Canterbury, *ten Copies*

Rev.

Rev. Stephen Weston, Edward-street, Portman-square
Miss Penelope Weston, Ditto
John Whaley, Esq. Wraxal Lodge
Rev. John Wheeler
Mrs. Whinfield, near Bath, *two Copies*
Rev. —— Whitby, Ditto
James White, Esq. Exeter, *twenty Copies*
Miss White, Ditto, *two Copies*
Rev. Dr. White, Wadham College, Oxford, *two Copies*
Mr. Henry Whitechurch, Tavistock
Rev. Walter Whiter, Clare Hall, Cambridgeshire, *two Copies*
Mrs. Wibault, Exeter
Rev. George Wickey, R. Marham Church
Mr. Stephen Willcocks
Mrs. Augustus Willett, Park-street, Westminster
Miss Williams, Exeter, *two Copies*
Miss Mary Williams, Ditto, *two Copies*
Rev. Jonathan Williams
John Williams, Esq. Exeter, *three Copies*
Mrs. Williams, *two Copies*
Miss Williams, *two Copies*
John Williams, Esq. London
Mrs. Williams, Bath
Rev. Antony Williams, Nansolven, Cornwall
Mrs. Williams, Truro

Sir Adam Williamson, K. B. Dover-street
Rev. Edward Williamson, Rector of Lolworth, Cambridgeshire
Rev. Vyvyan Willisford, Coryton
Rev. William Willis, Cirencester, *two Copies*
Mrs. William Willis, Ditto, *three Copies*
Mr. Thomas Willis, Bristol
Mr. Wills, Crewkerne
Edward Wilson, D. D.
Mrs. Wilson, Truro
Mrs. Wilson, Ditto
Bishop of Winchester, *two Copies*
Mr. Windeatt, Bridge Town, Totnes
Mrs. Windeatt, Ditto
Miss Windeatt, Ditto
Mr. John Winsor, Ashburton
Mr. George Winsor, Ditto
Rev. James Winsor, *two Copies*
Rev. Edward Winthropp, Leathershed
B. Witts, Esq. Nibby House
Sir L. F. Wood, Bart.
Rev. Mr. Wood, Milbourne St. Andrews, Dorset
Thomas Wood, Esq. London
Rev. Matthew Woodford, Archdeacon of Winchester, *two Copies*
Dr. Woollaston

Rev. John Woollcombe, Plymouth
John Morth Woollcombe, Efq. Afhbury, Devon, *ten Copies*
Mrs. Woollcombe, Ditto, *ten Copies*
Mr. Francis Woollcombe, Ditto, *four Copies*
Mr. C. Woollcombe, Surgeon, Exeter
George Woolcombe, Efq. Plymouth
Rev. William Wrey, Combinteignhead, *two Copies*
Sir Bouchier Wrey, Tawftock, *two Copies*
General Wrey, Barnftaple, *two Copies*
Rev. Dr. Wynne, London, *two Copies*

Y.

Mr. Morgan Yeatman, Briftol, *two Copies*
Rev. Mr. Yeatman, *two Copies*
Rev. Duke Yonge, *two Copies*
Rev. James Yonge, Puflinch, *two Copies*
Rev. Denys Yonge, Rector Weft Putford
Martin York, Efq.

ERRATA.

Page 13, line 2, for *is* read *are*.
—— 16, —— laſt, after *but* inſert *alſo with*.
—— 68, —— 1, for *attended* read *unattended*.
—— 80, —— 9, for *metit* read *merit*.
—— 91, —— 5, for *this* read *theſe*.
—— 108, —— 10, after *natures* inſert *of*.
—— 121, —— 3, after *is* inſert *in*.
—— 193, —— 20, after *and* inſert *who*.
—— 206, —— 8, after *yet* inſert *they*.
—— 248, —— 6, for *arrives* read *ariſes*.
—— ibid, —— 15, for *motives* read *notices*.

There are a few other literal errors, and ſome inaccuracies of punctuation; but as they do not affect the ſenſe, they will eaſily be corrected by the reader.

SERMON I.*

Acts, *Ch.* x. *V.* 38.

"WHO WENT ABOUT DOING GOOD."

WHEN we consider the constitution of things, our minds are forcibly struck with the connection which pervades the whole, from their infinite author, to the least important of his works.

In the natural world, the system to which our globe belongs, we have reason to believe, is connected with other systems, and in our own, we know that there is, as it were, a chain which links together its various

* Preached on the Anniversary of the DEVON and EXETER HOSPITAL.

various parts, and forms one ſtupendous whole. From the immenſe planetary orbs to the animal, vegetable, and ſmalleſt particle of inanimate, creation, nothing exiſts for itſelf alone; nor is this principle of union leſs apparent in the *moral* world. *Mind* is of one and the ſame nature, whether poſſeſs'd by Men, Angels, or God, and the operations of Intellect no more terminate in itſelf than the effects of matter.

What a glorious view does it give of the univerſe, to conſider the different parts of it as all depending on one everacting cauſe, and working in different ways by ſimilar means, to the production of one *great, good* end!

The connection which is thus viſible between the different ſpecies of the whole ſyſtem of the natural and moral world, is ſtill more viſible between the different parts

of

of the fame fpecies; and in particular, man finds himfelf united with man, in every thing which contributes to his prefervation and enjoyment. He comes into the world, even in a more helplefs ftate than any other of the animal race; he paffes through a long and feeble ftate of childhood, not only his body wants tender care and conftant affiftance, but his mind requires cultivation; he is plainly unequal to his own happinefs; he pines in folitude; he defires the fociety of his fellow creatures; and he has as *real* fenfations of intereft, in the concerns of others, as thofe which he feels for himfelf, tho' unhappily too often overpowered by the latter mifconceived and moft erroneoufly purfued. If fuch be the conftitution of things in general, and fuch the nature of man, what are we to think of his living for himfelf alone, of fuffering all his thoughts to terminate within the narrow circle of his imagined perfonal concerns, unmindful of the mifery or happinefs of others, neither weeping with thofe that weep, nor rejoicing with thofe that rejoice? what, but that he forgets his nature: that he is regardlefs of the great Author of his exiftence, who has fo forcibly pointed out to him a contrary difpofition and conduct?

Consider him as actually engaged in the bufinefs of life, in a ftate of civilization; (for to know what man is, I would not fend you to the *unnatural* ftate of barbarifm, from which fome would fain draw all their theory of human nature, tho' I need not dread the leffon you might learn even from thence,) confider him as enjoying the pleafures which belong to either part of his frame, his body, or his mind, as having formed domeftic connexions, as engaging in the intercourfe of focial converfe, as anfwering the calls of fome particular employment, or, if you pleafe, exempted by the bounty

bounty of providence, from *the neceffity* of following any particular employment, ftill, if he will procure for himfelf the moft exalted pleafure, he muft feek for it in advancing the happinefs of others; if he will promote his lafting interefts even in the prefent world, he muft make it his bufinefs to go about doing good.

Who is there of us that does not acquiefce in the truth of fuch obfervations as thefe, and reckon them among the moft clear and unavoidable conclufions, which the reafon of man muft draw from his nature and condition; yet let it not be forgotten, how little fuch obfervations were attended to by the generality of mankind, how little they were uniformly regarded, even by thofe who made them, either in the countries which were overfpread by the gloom of Pagan fuperftition, or the *partly* enlighten'd land of God's chofen people.

I have

I have no defire to build the temple of Revelation on the ruins of reafon; for I think it the glory of Revelation, that it coincides with the whole conftitution of things, and human nature, and that thofe parts of the information it conveys, which do not refpect the myfterious difpenfation of God's free, and undeferved mercy to miferable finners, which "the very Angels muft ftill defire to look into," are fuch as right reafoning from our nature and condition, might have led men to acquire for themfelves; but I would not have you forget, what the *fact* was; that men did not acquire it, becaufe their reafoning was not right, *unbiaffed* by corrupt propenfities; becaufe they had not a right knowledge of themfelves, or their condition in the prefent life.

Those fentiments are moft juft, and that difpofition in any literary production is deem'd to be moft correct, which appear to
uncultivated

uncultivated minds to be moſt obvious and eaſy; but it does not follow from thence, that on the ſame ſubject they would have produced thoſe ſentiments, or follow'd that order. Let it be remembered then, to whom we are indebted for thoſe pure notions of Benevolence which are ſo familiar to our minds, which ſeem *now* to ariſe ſo naturally on the leaſt contemplation of our own nature and our circumſtances. Since the Sun of Righteouſneſs hath ariſen and ſhined upon human nature, the underſtandings of men have been enlightened to perceive the common relation of mankind, "that we are every one members one of another." And their hearts have been warmed to allow the demands of their *relationſhip*, "to be kindly affectioned one to another with *brotherly love.*"

THE influences of chriſtianity are now felt by *all* in every civilized country with the

the dawning of reason, and first emotion of passion or affection. Its benign spirit diffused through the whole mass of opinion, and sentiment insinuates itself imperceptibly into the very texture of their minds and sensibilities of their hearts. Those who unfortunately acknowledge not, or ungratefully disregard its divine Author, yet experience in many respects, whilst they bow down to the idol, their reason, the meliorating effects of his unspeakable gift. And those who receive with meekness the engrafted word, and look *there*, for the foundation of their opinions, and regulation of their passions and affections, find in every page of the record of their faith, the most forcible exhortations to the virtue of Benevolence.

WITHOUT Benevolence, all pretences to natural religion, or revealed, are declared to be vain. If we love not our Brother whom

whom we have seen, we are told, we cannot love God whom we have not seen; and by *this*, said Christ, shall all men *know* that ye are *my* disciples, if ye have love one to another. Precept however is cold and unanimating, address'd to the understanding alone, which is too apt in the midst of a world full of temptation, to be overpowered by the will and affections.

HERE then behold the virtue of Benevolence receiving firm unmoveable support, and raising itself into the grace of heavenly Charity. Those who have a *true* sense of the miserable condition of human nature, from which we have been relieved by the mediation of the Redeemer, who are wash'd from their sins in his blood, and sanctified by the inspiration of his Holy Spirit; whose souls are sufficiently refined to relish the joys which await just men made perfect; who hope to join the multitude of *all* nations and kindreds,

kindreds, and people and tongues, in saying Salvation to our God which sitteth upon the throne, and unto the Lamb; who, in *all the* various scenes of life, look unto Jesus the author and finisher of their faith, behold his patient forbearance, hear his meek answers, and affectionate intreaties; witness his unwearied endeavors to redress human calamity, and render men happy; feel the immensity of that love which brought him down from heaven, to die the death of a vile slave upon a cross, and have the divine sound of "Father forgive them for they know not what they do," ever vibrating in their ears—Those men will have *every* feeling attuned to the love of their fellow creatures, and by the uniform *practice* of *beneficence* in their several stations, according to the power they possess, draw in *these* days the *willing* testimony from all that know them, which was once forced from the lips of a Heathen persecutor; behold how these Christians

Chriſtians love one another. The nobleſt object which our eyes *can* behold in the preſent world, is one of our fellow creatures poſſeſſing the power and diſpoſition to do good, and uniformly exerting it in the whole conduct of life. Let us then proceed to the effects of the diſpoſition we have been deſcribing.

Your hearts have often been delighted with the ſight of a well regulated family, between the different branches of which, there have ſubſiſted real regard and concern for their mutual intereſt: each individual comforting, and endeavouring to ſerve and pleaſe the others, and all looking up with confidence and love to their common Head, in whoſe affectionate attention to the welfare of the whole, they find a bond of union and an incitement to the chearful diſcharge of their perſonal duties. When in like manner, *all mankind* are conſider'd by us as *one* family,

the

the children of *one* Father, who has form'd them to live in focial intercourfe, and civil fubordination, who allots their different ftations, appoints their employments, diftributes enjoyment, trains them up here for greater happinefs hereafter, and conducts them to it, each perfon will receive his proper fhare of regard, according as he is placed nearer or more remotely in this great family of love, and from his fituation demands more or lefs our conftant and fedulous attention: in proportion as we are *intrufted* with his welfare and happinefs.

Upon this view of things, what are commonly confidered as diftinct duties, appear to have an intimate connection with the common calls of Benevolence, and regard to our own families; and the advantage of confidering things in this way will be, that our attention to both will be duly proportion'd; and we fhall not think as fome feem
to

to do, that unwearied endeavors to raife the latter as much as ever we can, is an excufe for the neglect of every other call for our beneficence. The truth is, the perfons who act in this manner, are regarding themfelves alone, even in what they appear to do for *them*; it is their *pride* or fome felfifh paffion, not real affection for their families, which they are endeavoring to gratify; of which we frequently fee a convincing proof, when *their particular* views in life are in any way *contradicted*. The mind which is capable of feeling real love for others upon *any* occafion, will feel it upon *all* occafions which call for the exercife of it; and the *fame* difpofition which leads a man to confult the happinefs of his nearer connections, for *their* fakes, will extend itfelf from the difcharge of every endearing duty of domeftic life, to the calls of friendfhip, acquaintance, neighbourhood, country, and human nature.

BENEVOLENCE

BENEVOLENCE supported by such enlarged views of our situation, will shew itself *uniformly*, and lead men to engage with alacrity, in *every* undertaking which seems calculated to advance the welfare of *any* of their Brethren; they will do their alms in secret, when the purpose they have at heart can best be served, by not letting their left hand know what their right hand doth; and they will let their light *shine* before men, when by seeing their good works, they may be induced to glorify their Father which is in heaven.

It is upon this principle, that we appear here this day, in this public manner; upon the same principle which has frequently drawn you from the comforts of your own abodes, to steal unobserved to the house of mourning, to offer consolation to the afflicted, and convey food and raiment to the hungry and the naked.

It

THE miserable objects which you have at such times beheld with *unavailing* pity, lead you thus warmly to patronise this public work of mercy. For often have you seen the ravages of disease, or the ruinous effects of accident, and no skilful hand near to assuage its anguish, and save the industrious father, or the tender mother of surrounding infants, from a premature grave. Ah, little think those, on whom pleasure, power, and affluence attend, what sights such scenes afford. And till men *have* beheld them, they know not the inestimable advantage of this heavenly institution. In a room unprotected, perhaps, from the fury of winds or rain, with scarce a pillow to support his head, or clothes to cover his limbs, without an attendant that knows how to *soothe the mind*, no food to suit a sick palate, or drink to quench his parching thirst, disease increasing, unresisted, or by the very means intended to alleviate it,

every

every terrible foreboding thought, haunting the imagination; in such a condition, present to yourselves one of your fellow creatures, experiencing that languor and pain, which *you* have found it difficult to support, with every assistance and comfort, which wealth, skill and affection could afford; from this wretched dwelling, see him convey'd to a place where he partakes of every accommodation his condition can require, every assistance the greatest learning and skill can administer, every tender attention which can contribute to his ease; comfortable in the reflection that all human means are tried, and thus yielding himself up in peace to the disposal of his heavenly Father.

I DARE to speak thus strongly of our House of Mercy, because it is so remarkably blessed, not only with the best professional assistance in the honorable science and art of medicine and surgery; but what can never

never be sufficiently valued or commended, the constant vigilant attention of many persons with heads and hearts qualified to guide this work of Charity with *prudence:* nor is it a small part of our glory or advantage, that these persons are of various professions in life, and different persuasions in religion; as it is the exaltation of this our *festival* of love, that they come thus solemnly before God, avowing their readiness to unite heart and hand in the service of their poor distressed brethren.

You, upon whom providence hath bestowed an abundance of the good things of this world, and the yet greater gift of benevolent affections, who upon the present occasion stand forth the avowed Patrons of this excellent Charity; on *you,* I need not attempt to inforce the blessedness of imitating your Saviour in going about to do good. You well know that benevolence, uniformly directing

directing the ufe of riches, exhibits what Job defcribes of his profperity; "When the ear heard me, then it bleffed me, and when the eye faw me it gave witnefs to me: becaufe I *delivered* the poor that cried, and the fatherlefs and him that had none to help him: the bleffing of him that was ready to perifh came upon me, and I caufed the widow's heart to fing for joy. I was eyes to the blind, and feet was I to the lame."

How are thofe men to be pitied, who imagine the advantages of a large fortune, to confift principally in the pomp and fplendour of equipage, and the uncontrouled gratification of their felfifh paffions; ftrangers to that felf-efteem and felf-congratulation, which *they* experience, who confider their condition in the light in which chriftianity reprefents it, as being ftewards to their heavenly Father, and whofe confciences
bear

bear them witness, that they are faithful to their trust.

But Charity is equally shewn by little as by much, when that little is given according to what a man hath: and an opportunity is this day afforded to all here present, of contributing *somewhat* to this Institution. If there are any here who have received benefit from it, and from a change of circumstances are able to afford some testimony of their *gratitude*; I do not ask such to contribute, for I am sure, *they* can need no exhortation to do according to their power.

You, who in better circumstances, have known what sickness is, (and *most* have known, and *all* may expect to know,) reflect on your own wants, your own wishes, your own feelings: as you have known, or hope to know what it is to *be pitied, so* may you now know what it is to pity!

Nor can I help reminding *all* here present, as well thofe who can, as thofe who cannot contribute to this Inftitution, that it is not *only* by their *alms* that they can promote the welfare and happinefs of their brethren: by difcharging, as chriftians, the duties of their ftations in life; by being good natured and obliging in their families—kind and affifting, and courteous to their neighbours—induftrious and confcientious in their refpective callings—by fubmitting themfelves in quietnefs and peace to the lawful regulations of fociety, and thus difcountenancing, in the moft efficacious manner, all turbulence and difaffection to government, the fure forerunner of general calamity: by *thefe* means, may they *all* fhew the benevolence of their hearts; and the *poorer fort*, by their fobriety and prudence, *preventing* many of the calamities relieved by this Charity, contribute *in effect* towards it, it, by leaving more for the unavoidable visitations of providence.

My endeavour has been to represent the duty of doing good to others, as resting upon the broad basis of the whole constitution of things, and the make and condition of man; as enforced, and irresistibly recommended to our feelings, by the precepts and nature of the christian religion, and the example of our Lord and Master Jesus Christ; as shewing itself in every act of kindness, assistance, and courtesey to all we have concern with, in various degrees; and as strongly prompting us in particular, to give our hearty support to such Institutions, as this day's solemnity was intended to recommend.

In a mind accustomed to consider the whole system of human duties in this comprehensive view, no perplexity will be occasioned by any seeming interference of different parts of it with each other. Modern Philosophers, as they are called, alas! how unworthy of the name! have most unnaturally separated the cause of philanthropy from that of piety and holiness, and affect to treat of benevolence, as if its dictates might sometimes be at variance with those of the gospel. But let those trying circumstances arise, which bring opinions to the test, and it will invariably be found, that the love of God, as he is revealed to us by Jesus Christ, (with its necessary consequences the regulation of our minds, and the due subjection of our appetites and passions to reason and benevolence, as enjoined by the laws of christian morality,) is the only true and consistent principle of the love of man. May a firm conviction of this important truth excite us to aim at uniform excellence of character,

to

to become more and more perfect in every good word and work.

IMAGINE then, my brethren, this bufy fcene at an end, and yourfelves able to view the whole of life through which you have paffed, *at once*, in all its circumftances, connexions, and confequences; fee yourfelves uniformly paffing on through all *its ſtages* in the difcharge of your duty, according to your nature and fituation, loving and beloved; behold good men dropping the tear of grateful remembrance on your graves; and anticipate the exultation of heart, with which you fhall hear *the Almighty Judge of the Univerfe* pronounce, " In as much as ye have done good unto one of the *leaſt* of thefe my *brethren*, ye have done it unto me."

SERMON II.*

GAL. *Ch.* i. *V.* 10.

" FOR DO I NOW PERSUADE MEN OR GOD! OR DO I SEEK TO PLEASE MEN? FOR IF I YET PLEASED MEN, I SHOULD NOT BE THE SERVANT OF CHRIST."

OF all the characters which the holy scriptures afford for our example and instruction, there is none (our blessed Lord's excepted) which contains a more valuable assemblage of amiable virtues, than that of St. Paul, and, what forms the foundation of them all, the motive of his conduct shines with peculiar lustre: indeed, the general tenor

* Preached at the Episcopal Visitation at Southmolton.

tenor of his whole life, as far as we are acquainted with it, appears to have been guided by the same high principle. Even when he persecuted the religion of Christ, he tells us * *that he did it out of a zeal towards God,* § *verily thinking with himself that he ought to do many things contrary to the name of Christ.* And although the public manner, in which our blessed Lord gave his gracious instructions, and performed his many wonderful works, leaves us no room to suppose, that a man of St. Paul's active and inquisitive mind could have wanted the fullest acquaintance with them; yet, when we consider the many and deep-rooted prejudices, both national and arising from the particularly strict mode of his education, which concurred in producing this determination of mind, we shall be unwilling to dwell on this part of his character; and readily pass on to the proof which he gave of the sincerity

of

* Acts, ch. xxii. v. 3. § Acts, ch. xxvi. v. 9.

of his principles, when it pleafed God, who was willing to fhew him mercy, becaufe, differently from his affociates, * *he did it ignorantly in unbelief*, to call him, in a more extraordinary manner, to become a minifter of the gofpel. A fimilar event is recorded in the new teftament to have happened to other perfons; and the difference of their behaviour upon it from that of our Apoftle, plainly fhews the different motives which influenced their conduct. § *When the band of men and officers from the chief Priefts and Pharifees came forth to feize our bleffed Lord in the garden, hardened as they were,* they were unable to withftand a momentary difplay of his divinity; *but went backward and fell to the ground*;—yet as foon as they rofe again, far from abandoning their wicked purpofe, ‖ *they bound him and led him away.* St Paul was not thus difobedient unto the

heavenly

---

* 1 Tim. ch. i. v. 13.   § St. John, ch. xviii.
‖ St. John, ch. xviii.

heavenly vision which appeared unto him; but having no bad motives to stifle a conviction, which he could not but feel, he gave up all that was dear to him, his fortune, friends, reputation, and national distinction and privileges, *counting them*, to use his emphatic language, * *but dung that he might win Christ.* § *Though brought up in Jerusalem, at the feet of Gamaliel, a doctor had in reputation among all the people,* ‖ *casting down* such *imaginations and every high thing that exalteth itself against the true knowledge of God, and bringing into captivity every thought to the obedience of Christ:* † *though after the strictest sect of his religion a Pharisee, an exact observer of the righteousness which is in the law, and a zealous promoter of it,* ‡ *preaching Christ crucified.* And from a more than commonly vehement persecutor of the church of Christ, becoming

---

* Phil. ch. iii. v. 8. § Acts, ch. xxii. v. 3. ‖ 2 Cor. ch. x. v. 5. † Acts, ch. xxvi. v. 5. Phil. ch. iii. v. 6. Acts, ch. xxii. v. 3. Gal. ch. i. v. 13. ‡ 1 Cor. ch. i. v. 23.

becoming its moſt faithful paſtor; the exacteſt pattern of virtue, and amiableneſs of manners, both to infidels and chriſtians; the warmeſt advocate for chriſtianity, yet guided by the cooleſt prudence; the moſt patient, perſevering, and, except in caſes that required an exertion of his apoſtolic authority, the mildeſt inſtructor of his flock; conſiſtent and uniform, taking care in all things that the miniſtry ſhould not be blamed.

WHAT enabled him to act in this manner, co-operating with the divine grace, which thus manifeſted its power in him, was his principle of action; which acquired ſtrength, and threw off its imperfections, as all good qualities do, upon his becoming a chriſtian.

FROM that time his ſole endeavour was to approve himſelf in the ſight of God; not
to

to gain the favor of men, the defire of which had fo unhappily mifled him; aware, that if the latter were in any refpect the ruling motive of his conduct, he fhould perhaps fall back into fome of his former miftakes, and foon ceafe to be the true minifter of the gofpel. In feveral parts of his writings he avows this principle and its importance: and fince in the text he has laid it down as the neceffary fupport of his conduct as the fervant of Chrift; it will not, I truft, be thought either unfuitable to the occafion of our prefent meeting, or exceeding the duties of the office affigned me, if from the paffage before us I endeavor to trace out the importance of it to the prefent teachers of religion, with refpect to *their* opinions, doctrines, and conduct.

And firft, with refpect to their opinions, it will produce inquiry: he who is perfuaded that he was fent into the world by a
fuperior

superior intelligent Being, who endued him with powers of examining and determining upon the objects which are presented to his mind, and that this Being is ever attentive to his conduct, cannot possibly think, that he acts agreeably to *his* will, when he permits those powers to lie inactive: certainly they were implanted in us by our Maker for constant use; and therefore not to make any or but little use of them, is, as far as we can, defeating *his* gracious intention: besides, as our reason is manifestly designed to govern and direct the other parts of our frame, such a person, sensible that he must give an account how far this has really been the case, will naturally be driven to inquire what the dictates of that reason are: and since (the appearances of things being frequently so different from their realities,) the result of this will unquestionably be a persuasion, that, in more instances than a few, satisfaction is not to be obtained at first sight;

fight; he will foon apprehend, that an inquiry into his opinions is not only a neceffary, but a very important branch of his duty. The farther he proceeds, the more fenfible he will be of its neceffity and importance; the more convinced that, in a matter fo interefting to his nature, and productive of fuch confequences, when providence hath afforded him leifure and opportunity, none of his opinions are to be exempted from fuch an inquiry. If this be in fome meafure the cafe of every man who has the free ufe of his reafon, under how much ftronger obligations to act thus muft *he* think himfelf, who is to affift others in their inquiries? who undertakes to * *teach them the difference between the holy and the prophane, and caufe them to difcern between the unclean and the clean?*

BUT

* Ezekiel, ch. xliv. v. 23.

But further, exertion of thought is no small labour; and however eafy a life devoted to ftudy and meditation may appear to the unexperienced at a diftance, it has been confeffed by all who have followed it to any extent, that, though flight inducements may engage men to begin, ftrong and powerful motives are neceffary to encourage them to perfevere in it. From hence it happens, that among the many who enter with fincerity and order upon a ftudious courfe of life, fo few, in comparifon, appear to make a confiderable proficiency. Obftacles arife which were not thought of; where they expected to run, they find themfelves fcarce able to move—their ardour declines—indolence gains ground—and whilft fome barely preferve the appearance, others turn afide to any objects that will attract their attention, and keep it without any labour of their own. What then is fufficient to counteract fuch difficulties? A defire of
fame

fame and preferment has, it muſt be confeſſed, produced wonderful effects, and, when confined within due bounds and in perfect ſubjection to higher motives, it is not apprehended to be forbidden by our religion as inconſiſtent with them: nay, as no one is at all times equally influenced by the beſt motives, and as worldly objects affect us more ſtrongly, in our preſent condition, than thoſe which are abſent and ſpiritual, it may, perhaps, when thus duly reſtrained, be willingly admitted, as what will add occaſionally a ſpur to the moſt induſtrious, and diſſipate the languor of the moſt indolent. The piety which is founded on good ſenſe rejects no aſſiſtance; her endeavour is to turn what is moſt unconnected in its nature with the purpoſe ſhe has in view to the attainment of it; and whilſt ſhe does this, ſhe only makes the *nobleſt* uſe of thoſe affections which worldly men abuſe: yet, whatever fruits have in ſome inſtances arisen from *merely secular* views, these, besides that, they cannot be relied on in any instance as an uniform and steady principle of application, on many persons cannot probably be expected to have any influence at all. There are men of ability and opportunity sufficient to afford hope of being useful in our profession, who have not the least prospect of rendering themselves famous, or of attaining, by such means, a station which can satisfy the most bounded desire of wealth. * *Now, tho' the persuasion, that even a* sincere desire to be useful, uniformly exerted, is not likely to procure notice and a due degree of reward, according to the common course of things, is to be discountenanced as unfriendly to the cause of learning and virtue in general: yet, to propose to such men *honours and wealth* as *motives* for unremitted application, would be to

---

* See Archdeacon Powell's 2d charge to the Clergy of the Archdeaconry of Colchester, in 1772, Page 4th.

to infult common fenfe, and to contradict the experience of the world. Some motive muft therefore be found which will act conſtantly and uniformly, and affect *us* all, as well as thofe of fuperior abilities. The love of truth indeed, arifing from a fenfe of its importance and our obligations to purfue it, is undoubtedly a fteadier principle of conduct, and in fome meafure level to the feelings and capacities of all men; and accordingly we fhould endeavour to render the fenfe of it, which we naturally have, ftronger and more effectual: but, in the prefent condition of human nature, who, that fpeaks from his confcience, will fay, that he hath at all times found this fufficient to withftand the allurements to pleafure and diffipation, which the common occurrences of life produce? What hope then is there, that it would be able, when once the defire of novelty is fatiated, to fupport men's minds in general, under

the

the fatigues of continued thought, and the perplexities of attentive difquifition? The difference of right and wrong, with a due fenfe of the obligation of the former and of our own imperfection, will lead the mind a ftep yet higher, and teach it to refer this, as every thing elfe, ultimately to his will who implanted this fenfe in us, and is ever attentive to the regard we pay it. And as we cannot but fee, that it is confiftent with juftice, that he fhould expect returns according to what he hath conferred upon us; we muft know, that according to the abilities and opportunities which we have, he requires of us application and labour. To this a conftant fenfe of every moment of our time being obferved by him will powerfully and uniformly excite us. Since, when once his prefence is duly impreffed upon our minds, we fhall no more think it allowable to pafs our retired hours in the futility of diffipated thought, than to fpend

the

the whole of our time about objects which merely affect the senses: conscious too of the weakness of our best resolutions, we shall naturally be led to offer up continually our earnest prayers for the divine blessing and support, in this as in every other particular of our duty, which we may thus humbly hope to obtain.

And as this principle of action, thus strengthened, will promote in us inquiry and labour; so it will most faithfully *conduct* us in our researches, and be the best preservative from error. If a man's first aim be to advance his worldly interests, he will be subject, whatever care he takes, and without any *wilful* deviation, to an *undue bias* in favour of those opinions which find the readiest acceptance with the great and powerful. He, whose grand endeavour is to raise admiration, will frequently find himself tempted to shut his *eyes against truth*, when she appears in the *homely* * *dress* of general opinion, and to *turn aside for a more unusual and striking appearance.* To agree with the rest of the world, and endeavour to elucidate received opinions, is too circumscribed a path for vanity; which will ever be urging on the mind to some uncommon pursuit, in which the rest of the world have no share, and of course can lay claim to no part of the praise. What a source of error this must be, it requires no pains to prove; but, if duly considered, it will perhaps account for many extraordinary appearances among the learned, which move the pity of every person of candour and feeling.

In short, interest will be likely to bias us too much *one* way in favour of received opinions, whatever they are; and vanity to prejudice

---

* See Sherlock's Discourses, vol. 3, ser. 3, page 10, 11, and 12.

prejudice us too much the other way against them. Now the person who enters upon inquiry under a continual sense of God's presence; and of being accountable to *him*, who sees the origin and progress of every thought, for his fairness and impartiality, is not in danger of either of these extremes; his great interest is to discover the truth, and therefore, with a due respect, becoming his age and abilities, to the opinions of others, he dares to think for himself. If he differs from them, should it be in important points, conscious of his own integrity, his chief concern is for their mistakes; and on the other hand, * *he is not discontented* or unhappy, when he *finds himself, after the* whole of his pains, of *the same sentiments with the rest of the* world.

Thus necessary and powerful then will the principle of acting from a sense of duty to

* See Sherlock.

to God be, with refpect to truth in general; if we apply it to the caufe of religion, of chriftianity in particular, we fhall find it no lefs beneficial and neceffary.

ALTHOUGH the two great articles of natural religion, the fuperintendence of God, and our accountablenefs to him, are the foundation of the principle itfelf, yet are there many other points relating both to thefe and others, which are fubjects of inquiry, demand labour, and afford trials of impartiality. And as the perfon we have been fpeaking of is already convinced of the attention which is due to the caufe of truth in general; influenced by fuch a motive, he can never think it a matter of indifference, in what light he confiders thofe truths in particular, which more immediately affect the object of his duty.

HERE

HERE then he will be careful to lay *well* the foundation of his religion, and not be likely to fall into any confiderable miftake; much lefs the fatal one of imagining revelation either impoffible or unneceffary: yet he will think, and with juftice, that what pretends to fo high a character, as the exprefs will of the Deity, addreffed to reafonable beings, muft come attended by fufficient vouchers to eftablifh its claims. This conducts him to the examination of the evidence of chriftianity: and his principle of action begets in him patience, fufficient to make a thorough inquiry, and fairnefs to examine well all fides of the queftion, before he allows himfelf to determine againft fo important a point.

WHAT the refult of an inquiry upon this fubject, thus undertaken and carried on, muft naturally be, need not be mentioned in this place; or if it need, I fhall not be
thought

thought unwarranted to declare, without any further examination, that it muſt be the firmeſt and fulleſt perſuaſion of the truth of the goſpel.

But here another moſt extenſive field opens before him, perhaps more beſet with dangers, and fuller of perplexities than any he has hitherto trodden. After the authority of revelation is eſtabliſhed, the next ſtep is to conſider its meaning.

The holy ſcripture, in which it is contained, may be conſidered in two points of view, as being in ſome parts naturally obſcure and difficult; and in ſome, though not ſo originally, as having been rendered ſo, ſince its promulgation, by various accidental circumſtances.

To proceed with ſteadineſs, and without prejudice, through ſo many obſtacles, which

the

the ignorance and paffions of mankind have been increafing for ages, and which they are ftill bufy to involve in greater difficulties, requires no fmall degree of nice examination, diligence, and impartiality.

THESE, however, (as we have feen) the principle under confideration naturally produces and fupports; accordingly the perfon who is influenced by it, having firft endeavoured to fupply himfelf with thofe aids from human learning, which are neceffary to overcome thefe difficulties, applies himfelf to the undertaking with ardour and ferioufnefs. Without abject fubmiffion to the opinions of any, however recommended, he examines for himfelf: but at the fame time, he is equally cautious of miftaking a love of novelty for a fpirit of freedom, and thinks it but reafonable, that a young and inexperienced mind fhould not haftily, and without diffidence, publifh and infift upon

its

its opinions, when they differ from those of greater experience; and especially when they contradict doctrines generally received in every age of the church: at least, in so important a business, he will wait till that fondness for our own productions, which the most disinterested are not intirely exempt from, is a little abated; judging, that if no less a space than nine years, has, upon this account, been fixed by a great * *master* for the private probation of a literary composition, it can never be prudent or decent to usher into the world our determinations of such higher moment, without the maturest deliberation.

If, however, after the fairest examination he can make, after waiting a due space of time, and revising and reconsidering the whole afresh, he still sees cause to differ from the opinion of others, though it should be

* Horace.

be in important points, he will think it both mean and diſhoneſt to conceal his ſentiments: ſhould thoſe points be ſuch, as to render a conformity to the eſtabliſhed religion an act of *duplicity*, he will behave confiſtently with the convictions of his conſcience; and, tho' unwilling to diſturb the unity of the church, ſeparate from her worſhip: in ſo doing, after ſuch care and ſuch endeavours to be impartial, he will deſerve the eſteem of every ſincere friend to truth. But, if (as I hope I may, without undue partiality, ſuppoſe will generally be the caſe of a perſon of our communion, beginning ſuch an inquiry upon ſuch principles, and carrying it on in ſuch a manner,) he ſees good reaſon to abide with that mother from whom he firſt imbibed the milk of the goſpel, having his faith and opinions built upon ſuch a foundation, he will attend to the miniſtry duly qualified

and

and duly fixed, *_shewing himself a workman that needeth_ not to be ashamed, rightly _dividing the word of truth._

This leads us to the second point, with respect to which I proposed to consider the importance of this principle, his doctrine. The person, who has from such motives taken so much care to have his own opinions well founded, will consequently think it but just to build those which he is to inculcate on others on their proper foundations; and as all his conduct has respect to the pleasure of God, he will, as a christian, esteem this an _indispensable duty_, lest he should be found to assume the character of being called _master_, in the strictest sense in which it is forbidden in the gospel. But then, in this, as he is assured his duty is to edify his hearers, not to raise their vain admiration, very different methods of proceeding

* 2 Tim. ch. ii. v. 15.

ceeding will be proper in different places, according to their abilities. To wife men he will **speak as unto wife men, requiring them to judge of what he fays:* to fincere chriftians of inferior capacity, tho' to them he will not preach himfelf, yet he will think a plainer and more direct application of the doctrines and precepts of religion neceffary; becaufe fuitable to the abilities and opportunity which providence hath afforded them. With *all* he will remember that his *bufinefs* is to preach the trnth as it §*is in Jefus:* though he will by no means omit to inculcate the truths of natural religion and morality, as far as they are difcoverable by our reafon: though he will call to his aid all the affiftances of human learning and philofopy, as far as his attainments extend, he will not, however, forget, that with fuch principles and fuch wifdom, in a very improved and polifhed age, men did not themfelves
attain

---

* 1 Cor. ch. x. v. 15. § Ephefians, ch. iv. v. 21.

attain to the true knowledge of God, nor consequently were able to instruct others in the way of salvation, which was opened to them by a very different, tho' not inconsistent method. *After that, in the wisdom of God, the world by wisdom knew not God, it pleased God by the foolishness of preaching to save them that believe, by §preaching not in the inticing words of man's wisdom: ‖for tho' the Greeks sought after wisdom,* ingenious dissertations, and sublime theories, the great Apostle of the Gentiles, and his brethren, preached Christ *crucified:* not *rejecting* arguments, brought from profane subjects to enforce their preaching; particularly, allusions to the games and other customs of the Greeks, (*as is evident* from the epistles of the former especially;) much less omitting to teach moral duties, as improved and taught by our Lord; but laying the foundation,

* 1 Cor. ch. i. v. 22.　§ 1 Cor. ch. ii. v. 4.
‖ 1 Cor. ch. i. v. 22 and 23.

foundation, where God had laid the foundation of our falvation, on the death and fufferings of *Chrift Jefus*. * Without this, a preacher may be a good orator, but he furely is not the true minifter of Chrift. Yet, as it is natural for the mind of man to go from one extreme to another, fo it hath happened in this refpect; and contrary to common fenfe, contrary to the general tenour and almoft every page of the gofpel, fome, from their zeal to glory in the crofs of Chrift, and to magnify his grace, have fo preached him, as if they were preaching to mere machines, and fo as to render him in probable confequence the minifter of fin. From both extremes, the fober tho' pious principle of our Apoftle, will be the beft prefervative: and as a juft regard for God will not allow his minifters to indulge, on

every

* See Archbifhop Seckers charges—firft charge to the Clergy of the Diocefe of Canterbury, page 235, and the third to ditto, page 299—See alfo his Sermons 1ft vol. 7th Sermon, page 150 and 151.

every occasion, in an oftentatious display of human learning, to the neglect of the momentous concerns of his express revelation; so neither will it permit them to suppose, that he has promulgated a law inconsistent with that which he has written in men's hearts, or with the reason which he has given them to enable them to find out his ways. In opposition to the enthusiasm of one party, or the self sufficiency of the other, he will preach Christ as he finds him revealed in the scriptures: and in conformity to the solemn engagement, which he made before God at his ordination, he will preach him as the author and dispenser of our pardon and sanctification, as well as the teacher of virtue; and principally on the motives therein contained, regardless of the scorn and contempt of the world, should different doctrines and different modes of preaching prevail, having this awful declaration of his Saviour ever fixed

fixed in his mind—* *Whosoever shall be ashamed of me and of my words in this adulterous and sinful generation, of him also shall the son of man be ashamed, when he cometh in the glory of his Father, with his holy Angels.*

But however just and scriptural a man's opinions are, however rational and evangelical his preaching, there is still a principal thing wanting, without which, neither will profit him or the public in any valuable degree. Good sense and experience of mankind, could teach Pagan philosophy to require virtue in an orator; how much more strongly does Christianity require it in a preacher?—§ *That those who teach should behave themselves holily, justly, and unblameably among them that believe?* Now a constant sense of God's presence is the only sure and steady support of virtue in general, and of the several particular virtues which belong to

---

* St. Mark, ch. viii. v. 38. § 1 Thessalonians, ch. ii. v. 10.

to the high calling of the minister of Christ: no other principle will either sufficiently lay the foundation, or direct and support us in the exercise of them. And first, nothing but an ardent love of God will beget in us that zeal which will render us solicitous to promote his honour amongst men, or inspire us with that steady concern for the souls of our brethren, which will make us really in earnest to secure their salvation. Other motives will produce an outward regularity, the true form of godliness; but this, tho' absolutely necessary, will carry us but a little way in our undertaking, unless it be supported by the true power of it over our minds, which can spring only from a real faith and regard to God, as he is revealed to us by his son Jesus Christ: this, properly fixed in the heart, will teach us the true value of our profession, and, as it is in itself most honourable, as well as beneficial to mankind, will make us esteem it above all worldly wordly objects, and according to the direction of St. Paul, *give ourselves wholly to it.* It will also preserve our zeal from dangerous excess. Religious zeal hath often been productive of misery to mankind: but tho' men, in other respects confessedly good, have been the authors of such misery; yet, in this respect, they cannot be supposed to have had that continual regard to God which they ought: since, had his nature and declarations been consulted with due simplicity of mind, one would imagine, they could not have thought such proceedings agreeable to a being of infinite goodness, and who requires us *to be merciful as he is merciful.* The truth is, perhaps, they, like other men, were rather too much influenced by the spirit of the times in which they lived, and had not learned, what it is the distinguishing glory of the present age generally to understand, that indifference and

* 1 Timothy, ch. iv. v. 15.

and toleration are by no means necessarily united. Tho' *we* have not now the *power* of proceeding to such extremities, nor should have their excuse if we had, yet a zeal not exerted under a continual sense of the Divine inspection, may hurry us into actions very injurious at least to the cause of religion, if not to the property and persons of our brethren: but when we have always in view the end of our conversation, party, prejudice, or hatred, will be likely to have little sway over us, and we shall proceed on in our course, *tho' as burning yet as mild and steady lights.*

Secondly, a constant regard to God will be necessary to produce in us proper perseverance; without this, the warmest zeal, regulated by the greatest prudence, will never attain its end: and there are so many things unfriendly to it in the world, that the means of supporting it well deserve

our

our regard. Not to mention the natural variableness or indolence, or the false shame of *our own* minds, the incapacity and inattention of some, the pleasure and profit of others, the pride and obstinacy of a third sort are opponents which it must continually encounter. When we have made the sincerest and perhaps most painful endeavours to impress upon the minds of our people the momentous concern of the great truths of religion, we shall frequently find no small number still ignorant and thoughtless, living without any rule of action at all. With others, immersed in worldly cares and sensual pleasures, less influence is to be expected; it may be, however careful we are not to give any unnecessary offence, some will be displeased with us, and count us their enemies, merely because we speak the truth. The pride and obstinacy of many is such, that, tho' they be not offended, and tho' convinced of their error

error, they would rather continue in it, than allow themselves to be directed by the knowledge of another. And perhaps in this above all other respects, *most* men have a sort of delicacy, which conceals the benefit they receive: nay, it is in some measure an unavoidable circumstance attendant on our profession, not to *perceive*, as in others, the good effects of our labour *increase* under our hands. The moral recovery of men is, for the most part, very imperceptible; and we must wait for the comfort of perceiving it, till it is gradually exhibited in the course of their behaviour.

Now, throwing aside all meaner considerations, if *seeing the success* of our endeavours be our motive of conduct, how soon shall we desist from doing any thing more than what we may be punished for omitting? If goodness of heart and pity for our brethren engage us, how will they endure
such

such continual disappointments, which will be the more severe, the more sensible we are of such amiable feelings? We must have something in view superior to either of these to animate and support us; or our generous feelings will daily decline, till at length they sink into indifference; and our exertions grow gradually more and more faint. But regard to God and our blessed Redeemer, moving beyond the sphere of worldly obstacles, will, in proportion to our ability, have the same effect upon us which it had upon the first preachers of chistianity. It will teach us to bear with slowness of apprehension in our weaker brethren, as God bears with our imperfections; and in this respect especially, as in others, * *to condescend to men of low estate.* § *As workers together with him, we shall not desist to beseech men not to receive the grace of God*

---

* Romans, ch. xii. v. 16. § 2 Cor. ch. vi. v. 1.

God in vain; but * *whether they will hear, or whether they will forbear*, to speak the language of Isaiah, § *add precept upon precept, line upon line, here a little and there a little:* remembering the warning of God to us by his Prophet Ezekiel, ‖ *we shall not cease to warn the wicked* man *from his wicked way, tho' we incur his displeasure thereby.* Yet, as the † *servant of the Lord must not roughly strive;* we shall be gentle unto all men, apt to teach, patient in meekness, instructing those that oppose; and, with St. Paul, endeavour, as far as our integrity will permit us, ‡ *to become all things to all men; humouring their tempers, and insensibly dispelling their prejudices, that we may save some.* In a word, this principle will carry us on constantly and evenly, ¶ *not weary in well doing:* for tho' we see not, to the extent of our wishes, the effects

---

* Ezekiel, ch. ii. v. 7. § Isaiah, ch. xxviii. v. 10.
‖ Ezekiel, ch. iii. v. 18. † 2 Tim. ch. ii. v. 24 and 25.
‡ 1 Cor. ch. ix. v. 22. ¶ Galations, ch. vi. v. 9.

effects of our labour here, *in due season we shall reap if we faint not.*

LASTLY, as the result of all, it will beget and support in us uniformity of conduct and behaviour, by which we shall, in the greatest degree, *adorn the doctrines of God our Saviour in all things,* and render ourselves truly useful to our fellow creatures: from the want of which, men, of no small worth, have caused offences to be taken against the cause of religion, and men of great abilities have done little good. Impressed with this constant desire of speaking and acting as in the sight of God, we shall be careful, in both, to have the true interests of our profession ever in view, never betraying in either, what may lower our esteem, or lessen our usefulness. We shall *not only* * *do no evil,* but conscientiously § *abstain from the very appearance*

---

* 2 Cor. ch. xiii. v. 7.   § 1 Thessalonians, ch. v. v. 22.

appearance of it; nay, * *take heed that our good be not evil fpoken of*; and labour to § *let our light always fo fhine before men, that they may fee our good works, and glorify our Father which is in Heaven.* "For this and this only, to adopt the expreffions of an eminent prelate,‖ will keep up in our whole deportment that uniform decency and propriety, which will preferve us from every unbecoming levity of behaviour and converfation; *add weight* to the dignity of our *characters, and raife us above all the common meaneffes of merely fecular men.*"

* Romans, ch. xiv. v. 16.   § Matthew, ch. v. v. 16.
‖ See Bifhop Porteus's life of Archbifhop Secker, page 90.

SERMON

SERMON III.

St. Matthew, *Ch.* xxii. *V.* 39.

"THOU SHALT LOVE THY NEIGHBOUR AS THYSELF."

It is evidently the design of the christian religion, not only to regulate the actions of men, but also to change and improve their tempers and dispositions. When this hath been effected by their sincere and hearty reception of the Gospel, and the gracious assistances of the Holy Spirit, (which is the perfection of the new birth, and the new creation,) all the outward expressions of duty

duty follow in due order and proportion. But whilst men are influenced only by external and distant considerations, their conduct will ever be irregular and inconsistent. And as this is the case of religious obedience in general, so the duties of each particular branch will then only be performed as they ought, when the genuine virtue to which they belong is seated in the heart. And with respect to my present subject, the relative duties, those which are owing from man to man, will never be discharged uniformly and constantly, until we feel for our fellow creatures the affection which is enjoined in the text: and if true brotherly love be really felt, the performance of all the social duties will follow as its proper fruits. I purpose therefore, first, to state to you the nature of Benevolence, by explaining what is meant by loving others as ourselves, and then to point out the natural consequences of this affection.

The Almighty hath implanted in each individual a regard for his own happiness, which shews itself in constant wishes and endeavours to avoid what is painful, and to attain what may conduce to enjoyment. And as it was his design, that a great part of our happiness should arise from social intercourse, he hath also given us feelings towards our fellow creatures, which prompt us to consult their happiness in like manner. But such is the condition of the world, that what will contribute to the good of others, frequently appears inconsistent with our own ease and enjoyment, to which our self-love is continually prompting us to have immediate regard. And this principle of self-love gains so much strength, by acting upon us continually, and by the indulgence of our early years, before our benevolent affections begin to expand, that it generally acquires too great a share of influence in the human heart. For at first we live the life of of mere animals, and gradually rife to that which is rational and social. It becomes therefore the bufinefs of reafon, as we acquire the power of confidering what paffes within us, and of directing the feveral propenfities of our nature, to counteract this undue attention to ourfelves, which operates to the neglect, and fometimes to the injury of others, by placing their feelings and concerns in the fame point of view, as that in which we confider ourfelves, and our own concerns. If *we* feel pain, we can confider that pain is the fame fenfation when felt by them. If *we* feel pleafure, we can recollect, that pleafure and delight are equally defired by them. The confequence of this habit of contemplating the feelings of others is, that we regard their welfare as we unavoidably regard our own, and from our focial affection, as really wifh that they may avoid mifery, and obtain happinefs, as from our perfonal affection, we wifh that

we

we may do so ourselves. In the degrees, indeed, of that warmth with which we regard others, and of that with which we regard ourselves, there will be in most persons a considerable difference; as there is in the regard which we shew for different persons as they stand in a nearer degree of connection with us, or in one more distant, as they interest more or less the other feelings of our nature: But as we may be really interested for several persons, whom we love in different degrees, and whose happiness, we consequently desire with different degrees of earnestness, so we may be as *really* interested for others, as for ourselves, whilst yet we love ourselves the best. You see then, I hope, what is meant by loving others as ourselves; it is entering into what concerns their happiness and welfare, as *truly* as we enter into what concerns our own; entering into it, I mean with our *hearts*, not coldly performing beneficent actions,

actions, which some would represent as the whole of Charity, as they represent the outward compliance with the divine commands as the whole of *the love* of God. But these men surely forget that the outward action affects our moral character, only as it is an evidence of an internal feeling. In this way of stating this precept, you perceive nothing extravagant or impracticable, nothing but what may reasonably be made a subject of command, nothing but what in some measure, tho', God knows, far short of what it should be, mankind in general experiences; and therefore, nothing for the minds of any to be startled at, as, I fear, is sometimes the case on hearing this command, from the want of considering dispassionately its true sense and meaning. You have also, probably observed, that what has been offered in explanation of this virtue, is true altogether, independently of the religion of Christ: And the reason is, that

that the feeds of it were originally planted in our nature by our gracious Creator, at the fame time with the love which we bear to ourfelves: and the religion of Chrift, gives us no new feelings, but only reftrains, cherifhes, or directs, thofe which belong to our nature. It reftrains our inordinate felf-love, it cherifhes and directs our love of our fellow creatures, and this in fo clear a manner, and with fuch affecting confiderations, as were altogether unknown before: it carries it to fo much greater extent, than unaffifted reafon could conceive, that the Chriftian love of our brethren, juftly deferves to be called, as it is in the Holy Scriptures, a *new* commandment. I proceed to the particular effects of this principle of Benevolence, reformed, exalted, and extended, into the Chriftian grace of Charity. It will lead us to rejoice with thofe that do rejoice, and to weep with thofe that weep. As the misfortunes of others will give us pain,

pain, tho' pain not attended by the comfort of felf-approbation; fo their fuccefs and profperity, will *really* add to our fatisfaction and happinefs. Perhaps, this is not fo often the cafe, as we are fond of profeffing, nay, as we would willingly perfuade ourfelves, but it is a fure mean of judging, whether we do indeed poffefs benevolence of mind or not. Our fympathy with others, in circumftances of affliction, is naturally ftronger, and not fo much reftrained by felfifh confiderations. And therefore, it is more common to find perfons who compaffionate mifery, than thofe who really rejoice with the happy. And fince we muft frequently feel pain, from the various fufferings of our fellow creatures, it feems that from mere regard to our own enjoyment, we fhould endeavour to counterbalance it, by receiving as much fatisfaction as we can from their fucceffes. But real fympathy is an active principle, and urges on the mind to

ftrenuous

strenuous exertions to promote the good and the comfort of others. It suffers not a person to form private and independent schemes of personal good, but whilst he is planning or pursuing what may appear to advance or gratify himself, it leads him to consider in what manner the interests of others will be affected, and if possible, to plan his designs for his own happiness in such a way, as to include rendering essential services to them; and it will also regulate his exertions by the importance of things: it will prefer the *real* good of others to their *imaginary* good; the good of their souls to their present satisfaction; the good of the public to the good of individuals: And on this account, it will afford a new motive for an exemplary attention to piety and virtue; by which the most good is done, in the most lasting manner, to the greatest number of persons. Nor will the benevolent man be inattentive to any thing in

which

which the *satisfaction only* of others is concerned. That politeness, which in the world too frequently occupies the place of charity, will allow men at times to say and do what they are conscious may give lasting uneasiness, at least to their inferiors, and to such as appear not to be of use to them in the promotion of their importance, their pleasures or their interests; or through indolence, to be guilty towards them, of inattentions which deeply wound their feelings, tho' they dare not shew it. And among persons of worthier character, it is not uncommon to see those who have a real design of serving others, in what they conceive to be matters of consequence, by little acts of apparent unkindness or neglect, or perhaps by the very *manner* of conferring their favours, causing to them more real suffering, than their good offices can ever overbalance. They do not consider, that human beings have *minds* as well as

bodies

bodies. The happiness or misery of this life, does not depend so much upon great events, which seldom occur, as on a number of little circumstances which attend us every day, and almost every hour: and this must by no means be forgotten by those who wish to be the true benefactors of their fellow creatures—but this will most certainly be *often* forgotten, unless we have for others that feeling, which places ourselves exactly in their situation. When once this becomes the habit of the mind, so as for it to be done involuntarily, as occasions arise, every feeling of others will have its due consideration; every person will have his due share of attention; every action in which others can be interested, will be performed, in such a manner, as will express the benevolence of the mind, in the most conciliating way which circumstances permit.

It is a precept of the christian religion, not only to be pitiful but also *courteous*. The world may teach the mode, the spirit must be learnt from the Gospel of Christ. Every true christian possesses that temper, which is the ground work of the character of the true gentleman. Observe him then in all the various situations of human life, heartily wishing, carefully planning, and sincerely endeavouring to promote the good of mankind in every respect, with uniform attention and kindness, proportioned to the various claims of kindred friendship, acquaintance, neighbourhood, and country—loving and being beloved.

There are, thank God, some to be found, who make it their business to " go about doing good," and who have frequently the superior merit of continuing to do so, amidst the ungrateful sneers of men, too selfish and narrow minded, to form a notion of their views,

views. Nor in order to difcover them, need we confine our fearch to perfons of fuperior affluence or ftation. Thefe indeed have moft power of benefiting their fellow creatures; and every beneficent action which they perform, every common civility and attention which they beftow, come recommended by fuch advantageous circumftances, that it is wonderful to fee fo many of them regardlefs of the comfort and fatisfaction of others, as we do. And when they exprefs, as they ought, by condefcenfion and kindnefs, a chriftian regard for thofe beneath them, attending to their complaints, relieving their wants, and foftening their afflictions, it recalls to our view, by a ftriking refemblance, Job's employment of his profperity, " the bleffing of him that was ready to perifh came upon me, and I made the widow's heart to fing for joy; I put on righteoufnefs and it cloathed me, my judgement was a robe and a diadem."

But

But in every station, in the pooreſt, and the meaneſt, will real charity exhibit its influence, in all the little offices of neighbourhood and domeſtic intercourſe, and even in the manner in which men follow the humbleſt ways of earning their daily bread. In ſhort, as the whole buſineſs of life takes a new character without the particulars of it being changed, by its being devoted to the ſervice of God; ſo every action of ſocial intercourſe, altho' it continues the ſame in outward appearance to the eyes of worldly men, aſſumes from this principle, the dignity of chriſtian charity. And whoever would truly enjoy the preſent world, may draw from hence ſuch ſublime ſatisfaction, that all the common gratifications from which mankind in general expect their happineſs, when compared with it, ſink into nothing. Let us then continually cultivate this bleſſed diſpoſition, the ſeeds of which are planted in every ones heart,

heart, by checking what is unfavourable to its growth, and cherishing whatever may encourage it. Let us moderate our estimation of this world, in which alone there can arise that seeming opposition of interests, which is so unfriendly to charity, by considering the little value in reality of those things, on account of which, we give up the delightful sensations of universal love, and condemn ourselves to the internal misery which is always occasioned by variance, enmity, and discord; and by frequently extending our views to that better state, in which universal love will constitute no small share of our enjoyment.

Let us not in imagination, much less in conversation, indulge ourselves in the pleasure which our pride is too apt to receive, from dwelling upon the misconduct or imperfections of mankind, either towards ourselves or others, but on the contrary, accustom

cuſtom ourſelves to obſerve the pleaſing features of their characters. One man will travel through a country, and return with deformities only impreſſed upon his mind, whilſt another will have found ſomewhat to pleaſe him in the wildeſt and rougheſt ſcenes of nature.

Thus alſo may every character be conſidered in different points of view, which will have very eſſential effects on our diſpoſition towards it. And when we experience feelings of an unamiable tendency, let us compel ourſelves to act contrary to the ſuggeſtions of the moment, the doing of which, if carried into an habit, will unqueſtionably influence the ſtate of our hearts. Above all, with our conſtant and ardent prayers for this particular grace, " the very bond of peace and of all virtue," let us heartily pray, and earneſtly endeavor to obtain that ſupreme principle of conduct

and

and difpofition of foul, moft perfective of our nature, the reverential *love of God*, as poffeffed of all perfection and the fource of all good, which has a direct tendency to refine, expand, and exalt our affections towards each other; contemplating his goodnefs as difplayed in the common gift of the fame nature, the common prefervation of life, by the fame fatherly care, the common enjoyment of it by an union in the various gradations of fociety, and efpecially in the redemption of the whole human race from one common mifery, and the communication to all of the fame glorious hopes; thus making us fellow members one with another, of that myftical body, of which Chrift is the head. And if after all we fhould at any time feel ourfelves but inclined to act contrary to the dictates of Benevolence, let us recollect the temper and the precepts of our bleffed Lord. On the altar of divine love which he has raifed,

let

let us lay our quarrels and animofities, our pride, our petty felf interefts, and hardnefs of heart—and there will afcend from it the fweet Savour of univerfal Charity.

SERMON

SERMON IV.

St. Matthew, *Ch.* xvi. *V.* 18.

"UPON THIS ROCK I WILL BUILD MY CHURCH, AND THE GATES OF HELL SHALL NOT PREVAIL AGAINST IT."

THESE words of our blessed Lord, to which our attention is directed by the Gospel of this day, could only proceed from a consciousness of his having come from God to establish a religion in the world.

On any other supposition, they indicate such absurd vanity and enthusiasm, as is hardly imputable to any man of ordinary understanding, and utterly inconsistent with that

that sobriety and reserve by which the conduct of our Saviour on the most trying occasions was uniformly distinguished. When Socrates was condemned at Athens, he reasonably concluded, from the history of his own country, as well as from the natural tendency of innocence and truth to prevail over malice and falsehood, that posterity would do justice to his merit: but that his notions of moral and religious truth would be embraced, and taught in his name under every change of human affairs, was too arrogant an expectation to enter into his mind; and yet, were we to consider the Grecian sage, and the founder of the christian religion, as vested only with human authority; we might perhaps, on a comparison of the nature of their doctrines, and of the circumstances peculiar to each of them, be justified in saying, that such a declaration from the mouth of Socrates, would not have appeared so extraordinary, as the words of the text, from the mouth of our Lord.

But our Lord knew that he came forth from God, and had power and authority to eftablifh dominion, and glory, and a kingdom, that all people, nations, and languages fhould ferve him; that his dominion fhould be an everlafting dominion, which fhould not pafs away, and his kingdom, that which fhould not be deftroyed. That the gates of hell have not prevailed againft the religion of Chrift, is a fact; that great obftacles have been oppofed to it's progrefs, is a fact alfo; that they were fuch as muft have prevailed in the courfe of caufes and effects, had it not been protected and conducted by a power all wife and almighty, has been often and fairly proved.

In what way this almighty power was exerted after the days of the apoftles, and how

long

long it shewed itself in an extraordinary manner, has been the subject of much dispute; but, as has been observed, whether we extend its duration to a longer, or limit it to a shorter period, nay, were we not to avail ourselves at all of the evidence from miracles, commonly so called, the existence and progress of christianity, notwithstanding every impediment, is in itself a miracle; and affords a proof of its divine origin, to which, from it's nature, the process of time must give continually additional force.

IF, moreover, those very events which were in their obvious tendency most unpropitious to it, have yet been the means, and, humanly speaking, the necessary means of bringing it to the state in which it now exists, the proof of it's divine origin, from the success with which it was propogated, will be inexpressibly strengthened; for it belongs to God alone, to bring good out of evil,

evil, and through a series of ages, to execute the gracious purposes of his providence, by the operation of causes apparently the most adverse to them. This last point, is intended to be illustrated by an enumeration of some of the chief difficulties, which our religion encountered in it's infant state, and continued to encounter till the commencement of the reformation, and by endeavouring to point out the good effects with which they have been attended.

WITHIN a short time after our Saviour's ascension, the animosity of the Jews against his Disciples, occasioned the violent death of the first martyr, Saint Stephen; and raged so vehemently against the church which was at Jerusalem, that all, except the Apostles, were scattered abroad throughout the regions of Judea and Samaria. No event could promise to be more fatal to the infant church than the early dispersion of its members,

bers, before they could have been well instructed in the principles of their religion. Yet to us, to whom the view of God in permitting this difperfion has been explained by it's actual confequences, it appears to have contributed greatly to the enlargement of the church, perhaps to have been effential to it's prefervation. Had the difciples been allowed to continue unmolefted at Jerufalem, the chief priefts, at fome moment favorable to their purpofe, might have enflamed the paffions and prejudices of the multitude, and, by inftigating them to the deftruction of the Apoftles, have at once annihilated the chriftian name: for though they had been obliged, becaufe of the people, to releafe Saint Peter and Saint John without punifhment, yet the popular opinion might turn againft the Apoftles, as it had done in the cafe of their divine mafter: but when, in confequence of this difperfion on Saint Stephen's death,

thofe

thofe who were fcattered abroad went every where preaching the word, and the people with one accord gave heed to them; fuch an attempt, however compleatly executed, would no longer appear likely to effect their object, ignorant as they were of the particular ends which the Apoftles were deftined to ferve: and this may poffibly account in fome meafure, for the Apoftles continuing fo long in fafety in that very city to which Saul was commiffioned to bring thofe bound, whom he fhould find profeffing the fame faith at Damafcus.

The reluctance which the Jews in general fhewed to embrace chriftianity, was, in a very ftriking inftance, eventually favorable to it's eftablifhment. If that people had received the gofpel readily, and their rulers had fupported it, the preachers of it would have immediately proceeded to propogate it in other parts of the Roman empire; this,

this, accompanied by fuch a change in Judea, would have foon alarmed the fufpicious jealoufy of the government; the rifing fect would have appeared fo formidable, that meafures would have been early taken for it's utter extirpation; efpecially as the indignation with which the Jews fubmitted to the yoke impofed on them, and the erroneous notions they entertained refpecting the Meffiah, were not unknown to their conquerors. But by the oppofition which the Gofpel met with among the Jews, to whom it was to be firft preached, the Apoftles were detained in Judea and the neighbouring countries; their proceedings were litle obferved, and lefs regarded by the Roman government, as no alteration appeared in the conduct of the ruling powers at Jerufalem: and their followers, being confidered only as a fect of the Jews, were tolerated till they had diffufed their doctrines into almoft every province of the empire,

empire. At length the attention of the emperors was rouſed, and the moſt malicious inſinuations were employed to exaſperate them againſt the followers of Chriſt, on one hand by the Jews, who ſaw the eſtimation in which the ceremonial law had been held daily declining; and, on the other, by the heathen prieſts, who in the prevalence of the new religion, beheld the ſubverſion of their own. During above two centuries and a half, the chriſtians enjoyed no aſſurance of eaſe or ſafety, and frequently endured the moſt dreadful ſufferings of every ſort: contempt, reproach, torments, and death, every where awaited the profeſſion of the Goſpel, learning and ſophiſtry were exerted againſt it.

Such, indeed, is the nature of the human mind, that oppoſition, and even perſecution, confirm it in the principles which it has embraced. And, as they never fail to intereſt others

others in the fate of sufferers, who give such proof of their sincerity, they sometimes, imperceptibly, create a prejudice in favor of the principles themselves, which can render men superior to what is so repugnant to human nature; accordingly it has been found, both in religious and civil contentions, that many sects and parties have flourished under persecution, and when unnoticed and neglected, have drooped and died away. We may therefore admit, that a certain degree of opposition was favorable to the cause of christianity at its first promulgation; but it is contrary to common sense to suppose, that persecution carried to such extremities, and continued through such a length of time, had a natural tendency to make men embrace it; nay, we may reasonably conclude, that some inducement, beyond the ordinary operation of the motives proposed in the gospel, was necessary to counteract such disadvantages, and to prevail

prevail on perfons of all defcriptions to embrace and adhere to it, as we know they did. But grievous as fuch feverities were to thofe on whom they were inflicted, and inimical, while they lafted, to the progrefs of chriftianity, they were the means of furnifhing to pofterity the ftrongeft proof of the truth of that religion they were intended to reprefs: for they occafioned the moft rigorous inquiry into the evidence of it, both by thefe who embraced, and by thofe who oppofed it, and at a time when any fraud or defect in that evidence could have been eafily detected. As no fraud or defect was difcovered, (for thofe who rejected the religion, admitted the facts on which the belief of it was founded, but perverfely attributed them to the moft improbable caufes) the fupport which is thus afforded to the hiftory of the new teftament is fo confiderable, that the greateft enemies of our faith have fince, as well as then, been forced

to

to have recourse to other modes of attack, instead of attempting directly to disprove the history; which done, the whole system falls in pieces at once, which not done, all other objections can be of little avail.

While therefore, as partakers of the same human nature, we sympathise in the suffering of the primitive martyrs, reason tells us, that God, who in his appointed time, will recompence those sufferings an hundred fold, permitted his church to be thus assailed by storms, to demonstrate at once to it's friends and enemies, the depth and solidity of it's foundations. Men took counsel together against the Lord, and against his anointed, but he that dwelleth in heaven laughed them to scorn, and had them in derision.

Another advantage that resulted to the christian cause from having been so long opposed,

oppofed, was, that no pretence could be alledged, with the fmalleft probability, of its having been introduced to ferve any worldly purpofe; and alfo, that it was preferved by this means, from being corrupted in its infant ftate, by political or philofophical maxims. The different fchemes of Pagan theology, were all introduced and fupported by lawgivers and kings, and calculated to infpire a more awful fenfe of their authority. Even the Jewifh religion, as it was to be confined to one people, and to fubfift no longer than their ftate continued, was eftablifhed by fanctions of government, though of an extraordinary kind: but the religion of Chrift, defigned to be coeval with the world, and to be preached throughout every region of it, had no fupport from human power, left it fhould appear to be in any degree dependent on that power, or to have been more
particularly

particularly adapted to one sort of government than to another.

Had the Roman emperor and senate at once become converts to christianity, and taken it under their protection, the interposition of God would have been less conspicuous; and we, who even now, in express contradiction to the whole tenor of history, have heard so often that our religion is only an instrument of state, should never have been able to silence objections of this sort, and should indeed ourselves have wanted that irrefragable evidence to the contrary which we now possess. At least, we should not have had so convincing a proof of the sincerity of the first preachers of the gospel, and of their having been actuated by no motives of interest or ambition. Nay, had the persecution soon subsided, since interest or ambition will sometimes lead men to encounter geat difficulties, where they

they have a profpect of furviving them, this might have been faid of the Apoftles and other preachers of chriftianity. But it is to be remembered, that though they were fully affured of the final eftablifhment of chriftianity, fince their Lord had foretold it, they were precluded by the fame predictions from any hope of feeing it take place. Saint Peter for above thirty years, conftantly acted under the expectation of a violent death, and knew the particular kind of death which he was to fuffer.

THERE is alfo great reafon to think, that the confequences which actually enfued on the converfion of Conftantine and of the philofophers, might have been equally occafioned, and with more fatal effect, had chriftianity obtained the protection of the great and learned at a much earlier period. Had not the church been rendered cautious by oppofition and controverfy, and obliged

to

to repel the cavils of its adverfaries, by ftating its genuine doctrines with clearnefs and precifion, the maxims and cuftoms of the world, and the inventions of fcience, falfely fo called, might infenfibly have been fo incorporated with the chriftian fyftem, that it would foon have become almoft impoffible to reduce it to its original purity. Indeed it is difficult to fay what alterations or interpolations might not have taken place in the facred writings, to anfwer the ends of ambitious and defigning men, or to fanctify the conceits of vifionary philofophers, had the fcriptures at once been given into their hands, and been diftributed through their means. Nay, had the Roman government only not oppofed the progrefs of the Gofpel, fuch an interchange of rites and tenets might have taken place in the courfe of an unreferved and amicable intercourfe between Chriftians and Pagans, as would have caufed them to appear but like different

ent sects of the same religion. Whereas now, the kingdom of Christ, unaided by human learning during more than one century, unprotected by human power during almost three, and yet continually extending its dominion, stands eminently distinguished from the kingdoms of this world; and the scriptures were preserved unadulterated in this state of separation, till they were so widely dispersed that any attempt to falsify them must have been immediately discovered, and thus we have the testimony of facts, that our faith standeth not in the power of man, but of God.

But farther; besides these external dangers to which christianity was exposed on its first promulgation, there was another, arising from within, which threatened to be no less fatal to it. Many of the first converts, both Jews and Gentiles, though convinced by the supernatural evidence which
accompanied

accompanied the Gospel, of its divine origin, retained prejudices so inveterate, that they endeavoured to interpret its doctrines in consistency with these, instead of making it their standard for correcting them. Nor is this matter of surprise; for in the reception of revelation, men are left to the use of their natural powers, which are exerted as on other occasions; not urged by an irresistible, or, if it may be so called, a mechanical force. But, under the providence of God, even error becomes subservient to the investigation and establishment of truth: for had no such false notions prevailed, or had they not manifested themselves till after the days of the Apostles, the epistles of the new testament would naturally have contained only direct instructions, and we should have missed the advantage of so exact a specification, not only of what the truth is, but of what it is not: an advantage of great importance, as might easily be be made appear from what relates to the opinions of the Judaifing Chriftians in Saint Paul's epiftles. In addition to the paffages of a controverfial nature which are to be found in the facred writings themfelves, we have many works compofed by the moft refpectable members of the primitive church, to which the fame erroneous opinions gave occafion; and though thefe may in fome inftances have been received with too implicit deference, they yet conftitute a very ufeful comment on the fcriptures, and, at the reformation in particular, were of great fervice in fettling the form and principles of our national church.

At length, in the beginning of the fourth century, chriftianity obtained the protection of the fovereign power, and paffed at once from the moft diftreffed fituation, as to outward circumftances, into a ftate of fecurity, opulence, and honour. This profperous condition,

condition, except during the short reign of one emperor, it enjoyed without interruption; and we cannot help remarking, though it is not strictly within the limits of the subject, the fulness of time when this happy change took place. For not long after, the northern nations made a formidable irruption into the empire, and within two centuries destroyed, throughout countries of immense extent, almost every monument of ingenuity and learning. Had christianity not enjoyed, previous to this unexampled revolution, some interval of prosperity, it could not have been sufficiently established to survive so mighty a shock: it did more; it subdued the savage conquerors who menaced it with extirpation; it was transmitted by them to posterity; disfigured indeed by superstition and corruption, yet with its records so intire as to afford the means of retrieving its purity in more enlightened times; and we see it at this

this day sufficiently flourishing, not only in the old world, but in the new, to justify the most implicit confidence in God's promise, that it shall finally overspread the whole face of the earth.

MAY not this dreadful revolution also, which desolated Europe, and involved it for ages in the darkest ignorance, be numbered among those seemingly disastrous events, which under the controul of providence, have ultimately proved beneficial to our holy religion. Sudden transitions from distress to prosperity are seldom born by individuals or societies with due moderation. The church, after having sustained persecution with such unshaken constancy, was unhappily seduced by ambitious views, and the simplicity of the scriptures was disfigured by the subtileties of a vain philosophy. The innovations of every kind which found admission in the course of the fifth century

century were so numerous, they were interwoven with so much art, and maintained with so much ingenuity, that, had the state of things which gave rise to them continued the same, it would soon have become a difficult matter to discover, and a hopeless attempt to reform them. But the almost total annihilation of learning, occasioned by the ravages of the Goths and Vandals, though for a time it aggravated the evil, conduced, indirectly at least, to the cure of it. It favored no doubt the success of Mahomet, and of the papal usurpations; but the superstitions on which these were founded, were fabricated by persons who presumed so far on the blindness of their contemporaries, that the first dawn of returning knowledge detected the imposture; suspicion being once awakened, the whole system of religious faith underwent an accurate investigation, in the course of which the errors of the preceding period, less gross, grofs, but not lefs pernicious, were difcovered and expofed.

It is curious to obferve, that as ignorance gave rife to fuperftition, and fuperftition to the moft defpotic power that was ever exercifed over the minds of men, fo the exertion of that power, in an inftance, which perhaps of all others is the moft ftriking proof of its preponderant influence, tended eventually to the revival of learning, and by confequence to its own fubverfion. Nothing lefs than the afcendancy which the popes poffeffed could have ftimulated to thofe rafh and fanatical expeditions, in which an object of no importance to the real interefts of chriftianity, was purfued by means the moft inconfiftent with its principles: they opened however a communication with Conftantinople, where philofophy and learning of every kind had found an afylum.

The fortunes of that celebrated city, confidered with reference to the fame fubject, are equally fingular. The removal of the feat of empire thither, to which its aggrandifement was owing, was a meafure fo contrary to found policy, that we may perhaps be juftified in attributing it to the influence of an over-ruling caufe. Without fuch a provifion, the light of learning would have been extinguifhed; it would have become extremely difficult, perhaps impoffible ever to retrieve the hiftory of early times, and that unbroken feries of evidence which has convinced the ableft and moft fcrupulous inquirers of the truth of our religion, and which its adverfaries will never be able to overthrow. Conftantinople, having ferved this great purpofe, feems to have fulfilled its deftiny; it became in its turn the prey of a fierce and barbarous people; but it is remarkable that its downfall completed what its prefervation had

begun;

begun; the affrighted inhabitants fought refuge among nations confcious of the improvement they had already derived from a tranfient intercourfe with them; they carried thither the precious treafures of antient learning; they were cherifhed as they deferved; under their culture the human mind once more began to expand; the fervice of God gradually became a reafonable fervice, it was difcovered that the caufe of truth could not be promoted by fraud, however pioufly intended, and that revelation, to be refpected, needed only to be thoroughly underftood.

The conclufion from thefe obfervations is obvious. That if fo many apparently adverfe events have been attended with beneficial confequences to the chriftian religion, we may humbly truft that other adverfe circumftances, which at prefent fubfift, (the long and extenfive prevalence of mahometanifm, the remains of papal fuperftitions, and the malignant fpirit of fcepticifm) will finally appear to have had a fimilar tendency. Hitherto experience has fearfully and wonderfully confirmed our Lord's promife in the text: His fpirit and his power ftill watch over and protect his church; and in due feafon will bring it to that ftate of glorious perfection of which the prophetic writings give affurance. When all the kingdoms of this world fhall be the kingdoms of our God, and of his Chrift; when all the people fhall be righteous, and know the Lord from the greateft to the leaft.

SERMON

SERMON V.

St. Matthew, *Ch.* xxii. *V.* 37.

"THOU SHALT LOVE THE LORD THY GOD WITH ALL THY HEART, AND WITH ALL THY SOUL, AND WITH ALL THY MIND."

As the chriſtian religion was beſtowed upon us by the Author of our nature, all its diſcoveries and motives of action are adapted to that nature—to the *whole* of its conſtitution. That we may be influenced through the regard which we naturally bear to ourſelves, our fears are alarmed by the denunciations of endleſs miſery—our hopes are raiſed and animated by the proſpect and aſſurance of an happy and glorious immortality.

immortality. And so long as we adhere to our duty, from the considerations which our hopes and fears suggest, we comply with the purpose of providence in implanting these passions in us, and guarding his laws by their influence.—But that obedience, which proceeds from *fear alone*, will ever be paid with reluctance; that which flows from *hope alone*, will be rendered as easy and sparing, as shall appear consistent with the attainment of its object. And accordingly that entire resignation of ourselves to the divine will, which is evidently required by the Gospel, will be very imperfectly secured by the threatenings and the promises which religion announces to us. Even persons of more improved tempers, without the influence of some higher principle, will be too apt to recede from the trials of duty, when it calls them to the sacrifice of present wishes and gratifications.—But to him, who *loves* the master, no service appears grievous: every command is obeyed readily, heartily, chearfully. And the love of God, as he is revealed to us in the Gospel of Christ, is that great, universal, and perfect principle, which unites in itself the noblest affections in the human breast, which heightens and gives effect to every other motive of duty, and has the most powerful influence in the regulation of the heart, from which our conduct flows. It is principally and eminently *love*, which must produce and support a constant and uniform compliance with the commands of the Gospel, and make that compliance appear to be our present interest and our happiness.

I will endeavour therefore to state to you the nature of the love of God, by showing upon what it is founded, and to point out its obvious effects.

One

One safe rule we may have, if we please, to guide us in this and in all other matters relating to the concerns of man with God; and happy would it have been for religion, if that direction had been duly attended to— I mean common sense. And this observation is equally applicable to those persons who have deformed the duty we are considering, by extravagant and enthusiastic raptures, totally unsuitable to the natures God and Man; and to those who deny to the Author of all perfection, and the source of all good, any affection of the human soul warmer than bare reverence and admiration.—Love is the same affection in kind, whether it have Man or God for its object; only, when directed to God, refined and exalted in proportion to the spirituality of his nature, and tempered with that superior awe, with which creatures, and especially sinful creatures, must ever contemplate perfect holiness and in-

finite

finite power.—It is always founded upon an opinion of excellence in the object of it: and when raised to its highest degree, this opinion of excellence is joined to a sense of kindness towards ourselves. Imagine yourselves well assured, that in a far distant country there lives a person endowed with every perfection of human nature, and employing every blessing of human life to the best and noblest purposes. Superior to his fellow creatures both in the natural and acquired graces of mind and body, exalted in rank, abounding in wealth, never indulging himself in any thing wrong, and constantly employed in doing what is right, sober, pious, humble, meek, gentle, benevolent, beneficent. Could you forbear loving such a person, tho' the effect of his virtues neither did, nor ever could reach you? Would you not think of him with pleasure? Would you not desire to be like him? Could you avoid wishing for an opportunity

portunity of shewing such a person some mark of your regard? and if you had an opportunity, would you not endeavour to do what you know would give him satisfaction?—Imagine now this same excellent person to be most intimately connected with you, to be your protector, your father, your friend, ever consulting your welfare and happiness, and continually conferring upon you important favors; by means of which you found yourselves passing on thro' life, not only in the midst of present comforts and delights, but with the hopes and prospect of their being perpetually increased; what feelings would then arise in your minds towards him? Would you not really and heartily love such a person? In the former case, upon the supposition of your having no intercourse or connection with him, you would love him on account of his excellence—In the latter case, sensible of his kindness to you, you would

love

love him, both on account of his excellence, and on account of the benefits you received. You have been before me I doubt not, in applying what has been faid of a *human* character to God, who is perfection itfelf, and the fource of all good, from whofe mercy and bounty you are continually receiving more than either you can deferve or you can defire. At leaft if you will do this, you will at once not only fee the nature of the true love of God, but find irrefiftible inducements fuggefted to you, to love your heavenly Father with all your hearts, with all your minds, and with all your fouls.

Of the perfections of God, either natural or moral, we can form no conception, but by collecting whatever is great, powerful, wife, beautiful, good amongft men, and adding to it all poffible extent, and leaving out all poffible defect. It is an object too vaft for the comprehenfion of the human underftanding—

understanding—too far elevated above the understandings of Angels. But it is an object as real as any object which falls ever so much *within* the comprehension of our minds, as the perfections of that human character of which we have taken a survey. Nay, without the real existence of such incomprehensible perfection as we ascribe to God, nothing great, powerful, wise, beautiful, or good, could have existed at all. But tho' we know not how, by searching to find out the perfections of the Almighty, yet of the effects of those perfections we *are able*, if we will consider at all, to form some notion; indeed not a *sufficient* notion; for the love of God passeth knowledge, and we can never be duly sensible of his mercy to his unworthy creatures.

From nothing hath he called us into being and made us what we are; given us

the

the various faculties and powers both of mind and body, with which we are furnished, capable of being employed to many excellent and valuable purpofes; placed us in a world abounding with objects fitted to afford us enjoyment and delight, with none but what may in one way or other contribute to our real welfare; made even our greateſt evils fubfervient in the end to our greateſt happinefs; his eye is perpetually watching over us, and his hand ſtretched out in our protection, notwithſtanding our ungrateful neglect and forgetfulnefs of our benefactor; and notwithſtanding our repeated provocations, he is ever pouring out his favours and benefits upon us.

FROM what are called the natural bleffings of God, let us turn our thoughts to the wonders of his grace: confider what it really is to have all our fins and defects forgiven; to have a clear and authoritative declaration

declaration of our duty; to be assured of having all our concerns under the care and direction of infinite wisdom, goodness, and power; to receive continual suggestions and assistance from the Holy Spirit; and to know that our mortal bodies shall be raised from the grave, glorious and immortal, that we may have our perfect consummation and bliss both in body and soul in God's eternal and everlasting glory. To complete all, let us look unto Jesus the author of our faith; view there perfections in human nature, and kindness towards us, in every thing he spake, did, or suffered. And now I trust that nothing further is requisite to illustrate the nature of the love of God, and to shew that that affection is founded on a persuasion of his perfections and of his goodness to us. And as to its being the prevailing sentiment of our minds, it necessarily follows from the superior excellence of the object to all others; and

the

the fuperior degree of favor which we have experienced, and which we are allowed ſtill to hope for, from him.

It is the want or deficiency of faith and attention, which makes the love of God appear ſo difficult to be apprehended by the generality of mankind. From a real faith and due attention to the perfections and goodneſs of God, that hearty and fupreme regard to him, which is called the love of God, follows in like manner, as love for what appears to us excellence in any human object, from an intimate acquaintance with that object, and experience of its kindneſs towards us.

I proceed now to ſtate to you the effects of this principle.

And firſt—He who poſſeſſes it, will have great ſatisfaction and delight from thinking that there is such a being, the author and supporter of his existence, who governs the universe, and is ever most intimately present with him. The consideration of God's continual inspection is to most persons the source of melancholy dread—and no wonder; for almighty power and infinite wisdom, undirected by goodness and kindness to us in particular, is an object which it is impossible to contemplate without the feelings of awe and depression; and such is the light in which God appears to those whose hearts have not experienced this principle. But what high and refined satisfaction does he feel who can lay open his every design and thought to perfect goodness, and sovereign wisdom, and power, and rejoice that there is a being of such perfections to take notice of them.

SECONDLY—From such conceptions o. God, follows a willingness to obey him in
every

every thing, and a thankful satisfaction in every dispensation of his providence. We shall not find any reluctance in complying with the divine will; thinking every exemption from duty just so much gained to our happiness. Our obedience will be ready and chearful, not extorted by the mere force of authority grievous to our nature; our whole hearts will be in the service which we render to our beloved master and kind father; as soon as we know his will, we shall hasten to comply with it, from feelings of esteem and gratitude; assuring ourselves that every restraint is from somewhat which would upon the whole be hurtful to us, and every injunction necessary in some way to complete our final happiness; nor will the dispensations of providence wear their usual appearance to our minds: for considering every disappointment and affliction as coming from him, of whose perfections and of whose goodness towards us we have so deep a sense, we shall receive it as necessary correction, and as wholesome medicine, to cure the disorders of our souls; and thro' the whole course of the changes and chances of this mortal life, we shall be fully assured that we are proceeding on, just in that line of existence, and with that degree of enjoyment, which will in the end advance the great good of the whole frame of creation, and our own personal happiness in particular. Thus we shall feel the reasonableness of those passages in holy scripture, which exhort us to rejoice in tribulation, and to be thankful for every thing, *good* or *bad*: for the time past, we shall be glad that we have suffered, and for the time to come, we shall choose to suffer what may yet be necessary to promote the improvement of our moral nature, and consequently must recommend us to him whom we love, and wish most to please.

THIRDLY—

THIRDLY—Another confequence of this principle is, a conftant endeavor to promote the glory of our maker. I doubt not but many perfons hear with furprize fuch declarations of holy fcripture, as whether ye eat or drink or whatever ye do, do all to the glory of God—*i. e.* order your whole converfation of every kind with a view to God and the promoting of his glory among men: but with thofe who love God, this injunction raifes no furprize; they unavoidably pay him fuch attention. It is the natural property of love when it prevails in the mind, to have continual regard to its object; every thing which concerns that object is of confequence. We imperceptibly form our minds, and regulate our conduct with an eye to what will appear pleafing or difpleafing in his fight; and it affords an high fatisfaction, to confider what we do as contributing to his advancement or pleafure. Love produces fimilar effects when applied to God: thofe who love him undertake and carry on their feveral worldly callings as his work, not with eye fervice as men pleafers, but in finglenefs of heart fearing God. They enjoy what comforts and fatisfactions they have as his gift, and are perpetually confidering what effect their whole conduct and appearance has in promoting or hindering the progrefs of true religion and goodnefs in the world. They are very careful not to do any thing even in their moft unguarded hours, or to fay any thing in their freeft converfation which can have a bad tendency; they confcientioufly abftain from all appearance of evil. Whereever fituation or connection can give weight to their influence, they exert it heartily in favor of religion; they are anxious to have their children and families in particular taught the true principles of our holy faith, and to prevail on them to follow thofe principles in their temper and conduct:

they

they let their light fo fhine before men, that they may fee their good works and glorify their father which is heaven. And they reap the higheft pleafure from any gratifications or accomplifhments which they may poffefs in a fuperior degree to the reft of mankind, if by *their* means they can render true chriftian goodnefs more pleafing and attractive in the eyes of the world. Attention to all this, would be an hard and irkfome tafk, and have the appearance of unnatural conftraint, without fuch a principle as the *love of God* operating in the heart; and accordingly it appears to the worldly minded no better than the effects of enthufiafm, and is accounted to afford nothing but melancholy fear; but it naturally follows from this divine affection. It is the fure effect of the cooleft reafon employed upon confidering *the whole of things in their largeft extent*, and it affords a pleafure to the mind which no words can exprefs.

For

For even the most common and most laborious employment becomes under its influence the source of satisfaction; it is in truth the grand secret which removes the insipidity so generally attendant upon all human possessions, and consequently the true way to the real enjoyment of the present world.

Another effect of the true love of God deserving particular notice is the sincere love of our fellow creatures. Independent of the tendency we have to imitate what we love, and consequently to follow the universal benevolence of our heavenly father, the contemplation of the divine perfections raises the mind above all the narrow views of self love, which counteract our natural feelings towards our fellow creatures, and opens it to the perception of every thing excellent in the whole compass of nature: and the sense of the kindness of

our

our heaevnly father towards us, spreads a peculiar tenderness over the heart; so that there is an habitual propensity to love whatever is amiable of any sort in our fellow creatures, and, where we cannot love, to pity.; hence we unavoidably become interested in every thing which concerns the welfare, the enjoyment, or the comfort of others: we weep with those that weep, and rejoice with those that do rejoice. And what will be the effects of such a temper of mind in all the nearer relations of life or in the common intercourse of the world, I need not mention: in every thing important or trifling, the behaviour will bear the unaffected marks of sincere good will.

LASTLY—The sure effect of such a principle thus operating upon our minds and influencing our conduct, will be a progressive improvement in the habits of real goodness, and a constant regard to another world

world in which our love will be perfected, and confequently perfect our enjoyment. The more we love God, the more we fhall defire and endeavour to be like him, and the more we ftudy to be like him, the more will our affections be fixed upon that ftate where we fhall fee *him as he is*; and from feeing him as he is, the more we fhall love him, and the more we do this, the happier we fhall be. Who can form the moft diftant notion of that exultation of heart which will arife from the real view to which we fhall be admitted of perfect excellence, and our feeling, paft all doubt, that this perfect excellence will be the fource to us of unalloyed happinefs for ever and ever!

And now how bleffed muft be the condition of that man, who finds himfelf going on from one degree of ftrength to another, animated with increafing earneftnefs to appear

pear in the beauty of holinefs before God in the heavenly Jerufalem; confidering this world and the next, only as different parts of the fame plan and conftitution of things. *Here* he is travelling, *there* he will be at home, like a traveller, enjoying chearfully all the real fatisfactions he meets with on the road, and following the neceffary bufinefs of it with alacrity, having however his eye fixed on the end of his journey, fo as not to be prevented from arriving at his home nor impeded in his progrefs. Surely it is not poffible to form in our minds a character more exalted and full of dignity than this?—any lefs troubled and difcompofed by adverfe accidents and difappointments? or any which enjoys the moft common gratifications of human nature with greater relifh, or has a more exquifite fenfe of the more refined?—Such a character ought every chriftian to be; fuch a character, as you have feen, the chriftian love of God

God will produce. Do any of you confider this chriftian love of God as unattainable?—It is only becaufe you have not fincerely and earneftly endeavoured to attain it. If you would accuftom yourfelves to think upon God as what he is, and truly endeavour to qualify yourfelves for thinking of him with pleafure, to love him would follow of courfe. It is not a new fentiment to which your hearts are ftrangers: you are acquainted with both the affection and the object of it. The love of goodnefs is natural to the human foul, and, however overpowered by the corruption of our nature, experienced in fome degree by every one.

It is only neceffary therefore to abftract the mind a little from the influence of external objects, and to encourage our higher and more refined fenfibilities; it is only to raife in our hearts the fame affections,
which

which we frequently experience to be raised in them by the amiable qualities and the kindness of our fellow creatures, by the contemplation of perfection itself, of absolute goodness.

Suffer no day to pass over your heads without recollecting the wisdom, power, and goodness of your heavenly father; without recollecting that this being of *perfect* wisdom, power, and goodness, not only sees you, but is ever most intimately present with you, so that in him you literally live, move, and have your being; without recollecting what you have received from him both by nature and by grace, the blessings and mercies you now experience, and those you hope for from him hereafter. Sincerely endeavor to correct whatever is amiss in your lives or dispositions, and uniformly to do what appears to be your duty; imprint the sense you have of these things

on

on your minds, confirm your refolutions and animate your endeavours; by habitual and earneft private prayer, by the attentive reading of God's holy word, (applying what you read to yourfelves) and by devout attendance upon the public offices of the church, and (with the affiftance of the divine grace which you thus will certainly receive) you will find the ufe of thefe means producing in your hearts continually a greater and a greater degree of the love of God.

SERMON

SERMON VI.

Psalm, ciii. V. 2.

" PRAISE THE LORD! O MY SOUL, AND FORGET NOT ALL HIS BENEFITS."

THERE is no quality in the human character, which we more esteem than gratitude; nor do we confine ourselves to esteem only, but are strongly disposed to shew, towards those in whom we find it, all possible attention and kindness: on the contrary, ingratitude raises general abhorrence, and effectually prevents any fresh marks of our favor.

If this be the cafe in the little concerns which pafs between man and man : if the fmall degree of goodnefs which we poffefs, leads us to be thus pleafed with a grateful mind, and to feel fuch abhorrence of the contrary,—how do the great and numberlefs bleffings which the Almighty has beftowed upon us call for our thankfulnefs and praife. And how difpleafing in the fight of infinite goodnefs muft that heart be, which is infenfible to them : and yet thofe bleffings which are conftantly and regularly enjoyed, are too apt to lofe their influence on our gratitude, from the very circumftances which ought to heighten their value,— their frequency, and familiarity. There are, indeed, men to be found of the moft amiable difpofitions towards their fellow creatures, who would fhudder at the thought of neglecting an earthly benefactor ; who yet altogether forget without any fenfe of fhame or notion of guilt, the great fountain of all

our

our happinefs, upon whofe mercy and goodnefs all that we have or hope for depends.

And the beft of us would do well to afk our hearts frequently, whether we uniformly retain fuch a fenfe of God's goodnefs to us as as we ought? Religion is too often confidered in a forbidding point of view, as filling the heart with melancholy fuggeftions and defponding terrors; but this is men's own fault, becaufe they will view it on the dark fide; let them accuftom themfelves to behold it in its bright and genuine afpect; let them exercife their minds in contemplating the goodnefs of the Lord; let them cultivate in their breafts the feelings of love and gratitude for the bleffings they experience, and then, to cherifh a fenfe of his fatherly love, to utter forth his praifes with joyful tongues from the fulnefs of their hearts, to regard him in all they do, will be confidered not merely as their duty, but as the privilege of their nature, their honor, their happiness—Praise the Lord! O my soul, and forget not all his benefits.

The benefits conferred by God on man, to which I will endeavor to direct your attention at present, are those which are mentioned in our daily service, under the heads of our creation, our preservation, and all the blessings of this life. Were it in my power to give you the most imperfect notion of the structure of the human body, of the minute exactness with which the almost innumerable parts of it, and all of them answering some useful purpose, are adjusted, and the manner in which their different operations are carried on for the ends of existence and enjoyment: no heart can be so insensible, as not to be struck with admiration and love at the wonderful marks of wisdom and goodness displayed in our formation.

FROM

From the body, let us turn our thoughts to the superior part of our nature, the soul: consider the various powers of the understanding, affections, and will, and, what results from them, that distinguishing moral sense with which we are endowed; raising our nature to such a degree of excellence as places us in the scale of existence but a little lower than the Angels, and renders us capable of the sublimest satisfactions. The power of searching out and discerning right from wrong, truth from falsehood, of directing our affections and pursuits to worthy and appropriate objects, and of receiving delight from self approbation, was intended to be the distinguishing privilege of man. And tho' unhappily, through the transgression of our first parents, and much more through our own neglect and mismanagement, our understandings are in a great degree darkened and imposed on, our affections disordered and misplaced on improper objects, our wills averse from what

is good, and prone to what is evil, and the natural fenfe of right and wrong becomes weak and confufed; yet, ftill the principles of true wifdom, of delight in goodnefs and excellence, of virtuous purfuits, of felf enjoyment, are, by the mercy of God, preferved, and lay the foundation of our recovery from this difordered ftate, thro' the gracious provifions of the Gofpel of Chrift. By thefe powers of the foul, we enjoy all the fatisfactions of thought and reflection; by thefe, a thoufand means of increafing the enjoyments of life are found out and ufefully applied; by thefe, we reap all the pleafures of love, friendfhip, and focial intercourfe; and by thefe, we are made fenfible of the exiftence and perfections of our great and glorious Creator, and are enabled to offer up to him that adoration and praife which chiefly diftinguifhes us from the reft of the creation: and further, our fouls are not fubject to decay or diffolution, but
when

when our bodies are mouldering in the duſt, they will ſtill retain their being and their powers; they are *immortal*, and nothing can ſhorten or deſtroy their exiſtence, but that almighty Being who firſt created them, and who, as he is unchangeable, the ſame yeſterday to day and for ever, we may be ſure will not.

CAN we now conſider what we are, with what wonderful contrivance our bodies are formed, and what noble faculties our ſouls poſſeſs, and not have the deepeſt ſenſe of the goodneſs of that great and gracious Being, from whom we derived our exiſtence? Can our ſouls forbear praiſing him for the benefit of our *creation* ?—But our preſervation no leſs calls for our thankfulneſs and praiſe.

WHEN the various parts of the human frame are conſidered, and the number of thofe delicate fibres, which are neceffary to the prefervation of life, and yet are capable of being difordered by the flighteft accident, we ftand amazed at the continuance of our being, and fenfible how unable we are of ourfelves to fecure them from injury, and even to guard againft the external annoyances to which we are expofed; we are led to acknowledge with the utmoft lowlinefs, that it is through the Lord that we have been holden up ever fince we were born, and that he only can make us dwell in fafety. And this is the cafe not merely with refpect to our bodies, but the health and peace of our fouls alfo depend upon the fupport of God's providence. If we have ever feen the moft melancholy fpectacle which human eyes can behold—one of our fellow creatures deprived of the due ufe of his reafon, we fhall not need any arguments to convince us how ineftimable a bleffing it is to poffefs a found mind, altho, like the

bleffing

bleffing of bodily health, it be but little confidered by the generality of mankind. The fame in proportion is true of all the other faculties of our fouls; on God's fupport they all depend: were that withdrawn for a moment, confufion would enfue. But our gracious Father's goodnefs fhews itfelf alfo in the manner in which our being is continued to us.

This globe upon which we are placed, is furnifhed not only with things neceffary for our fupport, but with numberlefs comforts and delights; indeed there is fcarce an object which ferves barely for ufe, and has not in fome degree the power of affording us pleafure: we feldom confider, perhaps, how much the goodnefs of God is manifeft in the pleafure which attends our taking in our daily food; in the prevalence of agreeable fmells over thofe which are difagreeable; of harmonious and fweet

founds

sounds above those which offend the ear; in surfaces which are pleasing to the touch; and in the effects of light and colour on the sight. We can easily imagine how all the purposes necessary to our existence might have been attained, without those agreeable sensations which are annexed to them, and must therefore allow those pleasing circumstances to be an additional proof of the goodness of God. Our daily food might have equally supported us, tho' it had the same effect upon our palate as the most nauseous medicine; our smell might have served to assist us in discovering the qualities of things, tho' we had never been gratified with the scent of the rose; the necessary purposes of hearing had been answered, tho' every tone of the human voice, every sound uttered by bird or beast or occasioned by inanimate things, had been harsh and grating; our feeling might have contributed to secure us from injury, and assisted us to

form

form juft notions of the fize and fhape of things, tho' the touch of the fofteft down had been like that of the rougheft ftone; and our eyes might have given us every requifite benefit of fight, tho' we had never viewed the glory of the fun, the majeftic grandeur of the heavens, the varied verdure of the landfcape, or the ftupendous expanfe of the ocean; in fhort every neceffary purpofe of the productions of nature might have been effected for our exiftence without thofe various fources of delight with which they are accompanied.

If from the natural productions of God's providence for our being and welfare, we afcend to the confideration of focial intercourfe; of the affiftances and pleafures which we receive from the various arrangements of regular government and civil fubordination; how the combined powers of mind and body, of intellect and ftrength are

are duly exerted in the promotion of general security, order, and happiness; how our affections are softened and improved; how every faculty of the human soul is drawn forth and exercised on its suitable object: the hidden properties of the animal, vegetable, and natural world, searched out and applied to the uses to which they are adapted; how we reap from them by far the greatest part of the refined delights which spring from the several connections of life, of marriage, kindred, friendship, and acquaintance; unless with some of modern times, we find the origin of all these blessings in an imaginary agreement of savages, we shall still further adore the goodness of our Creator, who not only formed man for society, but actually, if at least we may believe his holy word, placed him in a state of civil subordination; what a happy creature even in the present world might man be, if he knew and considered the

blessings

blessings he has received! But too often, from equal infatuation and ingratitude, does he look only on the unpleasing part of his condition; he abuses the advantages he cannot but see, and even turns them to his hurt; the various powers of a superior nature he employs in counteracting that order which his maker has established, and of consequence, in producing to himself in the end unhappiness; all the natural delights with which this world is furnished he seizes on, in such a disproportionate manner, as to destroy even the power of enjoyment; the purposes of civil life he perverts under the instigations of unruly passions, to cruelty, bloodshed, and confusion; and were he left to himself, (did not our heavenly Father still interfere to guide and controul him, as far as is consistent with due freedom of will,) how soon would this world, which was intended for his rational enjoyment and comfort, become a

scene

scene of continued misery: what compleats therefore the goodness of God in the preservation to us of our being is, his directing us by his fatherly hand, in our progress thro' life, in which he has placed us, and in our enjoyment of the blessings he has bestowed.

It is indeed beyond the reach of our capacity to discover how this is continually done: yet our reason and the express declarations of scripture lead us to a firm belief of God's overuling providence, and to an entire resignation of ourselves and all our concerns, whilst we humbly endeavour to do for ourselves what we can, to his infinite wisdom, power, and goodness; assured that he will give us such a degree of enjoyment as shall be most conducive to our lasting happiness—and what more can we desire? It is true, in the various succession of events, he often sends, even to those who trust in him, disappointments and sufferings, but always

always with a merciful defign; to punifh in order to amend us and others, to perfect in us what will produce greater happinefs; to draw our eyes towards that bleffed place where his fatherly kindnefs will fhine with its brighteft luftre, not clouded by thofe acts of feverity which are needful in this our ftate of education. But amidft all thefe, what numberlefs comforts do we poffefs beyond our higheft deferts: fome perfons indeed are more liberally furnifhed with the favours of providence than others; undoubtedly for the wifeft and beft reafons, known only to him who is equally the father of all men, and who has a right to do what he pleafes with his own. But all of us, if we would attentively and impartially look back upon the events of our paft lives, might fee and feel how gracious the Lord hath been unto us.

LET

LET us take a view of our real conditions, laying aside pride and all undue pretensions, and we shall soon become sensible, not only how little reason we have upon the whole to complain, but how great reason we have to be thankful. The mercy of God is over all his works, and, except to the incorrigible offender, in every event which befalls us; but were it in no event but one, which comes not within the subject of this discourse, but which gives in fact, by the cheering hope it affords, true value to all the rest: were the riches of God's mercy experienced solely in sending his only begotten and eternal son to die for us, the just for the unjust; this alone might well swallow up every other consideration; and amidst all the anxieties, disappointments, and sufferings of this short transitory life, fill our hearts with joyful hope of that glory which shall be revealed, and with thankful gratitude for our deliverance from that

that misery which has no end and no intermission: but **God's** goodness is unbounded, and this stupendous instance so far from exhausting it, is an earnest to us of every other: He that spared not his own son, but gave him up for us all; how shall he not with him also freely give us all things?

LET us look at ourselves, then within and without; and whilst our minds are struck with the wonderful wisdom and contrivance so conspicuous in the formation and constitution both of our bodies and our souls, let not the goodness of our Maker which is equally conspicuous pass unregarded; whilst we contemplate this fair temple in which he has appointed us to dwell, and our hearts swell within us on beholding the sky, air, earth, and heaven, let the fulness of them burst forth in the warmest acclamations of praise to the gracious Lord of all: when we view the delightful productions of man's skill and labor, or feel within us still more refined and animating emotions, the conjugal, the parental, the filial, the friendly, the social, the humane; let us recollect what we owe to the King of Kings, and Lord of Lords, who has established the beautiful order of civil subordination, under which alone they can be duly enjoyed, and appointed our lot under a constitution of government in Church and State, and in a period of society the most favorable to every virtuous enjoyment of our nature, and the highest perfection of the human character.

AND in the more retired paths of private life, if any of us should be disposed to fix his thoughts solely on what is less pleasing in his condition; let him turn to the opposite and more satisfying view; consider the many comforts which attend almost every situation, and make the best use of them

them, by enjoying them as his Maker intended. He will then foon be fenfible of the divine goodnefs in what cannot but be grievous to human nature, and upon the whole, with fuch views, reap more real fatisfaction in the midft of affliction, than an irreligious man, whofe views extend not beyond what ftrikes his fenfes, ever enjoyed in the height of profperity.

ABOVE all things, let us conftantly pray to God through the interceffion of our Redeemer, that to the bleffings which he is continually pouring out upon us, he will be pleafed to annex, what crowns and perfects all his gifts to man in this world—a grateful heart—" to tafte thofe gifts with joy."

SERMON VII.

Psalm, ciii. V. 2.

"PRAISE THE LORD! O MY SOUL, AND FORGET NOT ALL HIS BENEFITS."

THE creation and preservation of the world, with all the comforts and conveniencies of life, are benefits which it might well be supposed men could not be in any danger of forgetting; but experience teaches us that the case is very far otherwise: and God our creator and preserver, and who giveth us all things richly to enjoy, is too often not in all our thoughts, whilst

whilſt we feel and perhaps acknowledge the moſt grateful ſenſe of the inferior benefits which we have received from our fellow creatures.

To recall our attention to thoſe ſubjects is therefore neceſſary, and has been attempted in a preceding diſcourſe. But the bleſſings of creation and preſervation, great as they are, only lead to the conſideration of another ſtill more important to us *miſerable ſinners*.

For how much better would it have been for us never to have exiſted, than to have received this bleſſing only to render ourſelves the objects of God's diſpleaſure; how much better, were it poſſible, to loſe our exiſtence, than to live on here for a ſhort time in a ſtate of ſolicitude and anxiety, and then leave all we hold dear, to become partakers of that juſt condemnation which

which we have deferved: fo much is the bleffing of our *redemption* of more importance to us than our creation or our prefervation.

The relations in which God ftands to us of creator and preferver, lay us under the obligation of conforming ourfelves to his will: if we *have* done and continue to do this, we have nothing to fear, but may *affure* ourfelves, that infinite juftice will never fuffer our being to be worfe to us than *not* being, and may hope that infinite goodnefs will preferve to us (if not increafe) the bleffings we enjoy; in this cafe we have no further to look, and a *Redeemer* is upon this fuppofition altogether unneceffary; but are we thus *innocent*—thus *perfect?* *Far* be from us the arrogant imagination; we know, we *feel* that we have been and are finners, in thought, word, and deed: we have, in the expreffive words of our Liturgy,
erred

erred and strayed from God's ways like lost sheep; we have followed too much the devices and desires of our own hearts; we have offended against his holy laws; we have *left* undone those things which we ought to have done, and we have done those things which we ought *not* to have done, and there is *no health* in us.

FROM God's *justice* therefore, we have nothing to expect but punishment; from his *goodness*, the first thing we have to hope for, is *forgiveness*. But how know we that it is consistent with his justice, so to exert his goodness as to grant us this forgiveness? Let not the pride of human reason hastily answer *this* question, without having *duly* considered what the purposes of universal government over rational creatures *may* require. In human governments we find that the welfare of society cannot be maintained without the *punishment* of offenders; how *know* we that the fame is not the cafe in God's kingdom? and then what muft become of us? Undoubtedly to a fincere penitent, reafon and nature dictate hope of God's mercy; but hope mixed with fear, if matters be thoroughly confidered; becaufe reafon cannot find a fure foundation on which to build that hope; and if matters be *not thoroughly* confidered, the forebodings of confcience will at times alarm the breaft with anxious doubts; for ceafing to do evil does not undo the evil that has been done, any more than ceafing to contract *new* debts difcharges the old: but the advocates for the fufficiency of human reafon, without the affiftance of Revelation, muft be reminded, that even the confcioufnefs of guilt, (after the heart has been hardened through the deceitfulnefs of fin) which produces true contrition, and leadeth to real and fincere repentance, is looked for in vain in untaught and unaffifted nature; and

and if *this* could be there found, it cannot be found accompanied by *thorough* and *perfect* amendment of heart and life; for it is not thus found in *us* who are blessed with superior information, and are trained up to an higher sense of duty; *our* hearts condemn us of falling *constantly* short of the glory of God; and God is greater than our hearts and knoweth all things.

How then can *man* be justified with God? or how can he be clean that is born of a woman? Behold even to the moon and it *shineth* not; the stars are not *pure* in his sight; how much less man that is a worm, and the son of man that is a worm! To whom then can we look for comfort, and upon what can we ground our hope of mercy: blessed be God! there is one to whom we may look in this distress of nature; to him who hath pronounced with authority—Comfort ye, comfort ye, my people,

people, speak ye comfortably to Jerusalem, and cry unto her that her warfare is accomplished, that her iniquity is pardoned: blessed be God for the light which hath shined upon the people which walked in darkness and the shadow of death. We can now ground our hope of pardon upon the surest foundation; upon him who speaketh in righteousness and is mighty to save. Christ hath redeemed us from the curse of the law, being made a curse for us; for God was in Christ, reconciling the world unto himself, and made peace through *the blood of his cross*. Who then shall lay any thing to the charge of God's elect? It is God that justifieth, who is he that condemneth? It is Christ that died, yea rather that is risen again, who is even at the right hand of God, who also maketh intercession for us. Let then the proud disputer of this world trust if he will to the faint glimmering of natural reason; we

will

will be more humble, we know ourselves, and glory in the *cross of Christ*.

ONLY let us walk worthy of the vocation with which we are called, and receive not the grace of God in vain; for better had it been for us not to have known the way of righteousness, than after we have known it to turn, through wilfulness or negligence, from the holy commandment delivered unto us. That grace of God which thus bringeth salvation, requires from us as a qualification for receiving its *final* effects, sincere endeavors to attain universal holiness in heart and life, without which no one *can* see the Lord. And the way to attain this, viz. by denying ungodliness and worldly lusts, and living soberly, righteously, and godly in the present world, is so clearly pointed out, so recommended by example, and so enforced by the most awful sanctions, that men must wilfully

shut

shut their eyes and harden their hearts if they do not see and be converted. And that no encouragement may be wanting, it is the great and diſtinguiſhing excellence of the chriſtian religion, that it not only gives us the aſſurance of pardon for our paſt ſins, but promiſes every requiſite aſſiſtance to our ſincere endeavors for the time to come. This doctrine of holy ſcripture hath not been by ſome of late years valued as it ought to be, from the miſtakes reſpecting it, into which ſome ill informed tho' well meaning perſons have fallen, thinking to exalt the glory of the Redeemer by diſparaging the original work of his hand. For in holy ſcripture, the creation of man at firſt, is as expreſſly aſcribed to the eternal Son of God, as our redemption; and perhaps the circumſtance of its being ſo familiar to our minds, prevents its affecting us in the way it otherwiſe would. But let not the too high ſenſe of the efficacy of

divine

divine grace, which other perfons may have entertained, lead us to undervalue its neceffity and importance.

For what are *we* with all the information we have received refpecting our condition and God's purpofes of mercy, if left to ourfelves. If God by his holy fpirit did not ftill work in us both to will and to do, confiftently indeed with the free agency of creatures in a ftate of moral probation and difcipline. But let us imagine to ourfelves, that with a due confcioufnefs of our own weaknefs and infufficiency, with frequent experience of the deceitful nature of fin and the power of temptation, and with a perfuafion of the abfolute neceffity of obedience to the commands and conformity to the example of our Lord and Saviour, as propofed to us in the Gofpel, that we were this day informed for the firft time, upon the indifputable authority of eternal truth,

truth, that we should become the temple of Almighty God, that he would come and make his abode with us, and that by his gracious presence and influence he would enlighten our understandings, correct and sanctify our wills, and guard, direct, and exalt our hearts and affections; with what holy consolation, with what awful gratitude would our hearts be filled! Let not then our sense of God's goodness be lessened by our more intimate knowledge of its effects.

And whilst we carefully avoid the errors of enthusiasm, let us not fall into the delusions of pride, nor forget in whom standeth our help; whilst we make the attainment of true and substantial godliness, in the most extensive sense of the word, the first object of our endeavors, as it is the only foundation of real happiness in this life as well as in the world to come, exerting all the

powers

powers of our nature in the purfuit of it; let us rely for the fuccefs of our exertions (and experience will foon teach us that we *cannot* find any other dependance) upon the encouraging promifes which are made us in the gofpel of Chrift, of grace to help in time of need. Not that with our beft endeavors we may hope to be rendered perfect in goodnefs, notwithftanding our daily progrefs in it; for abfolute perfection is not the lot of man on earth, or angels in heaven; his very angels he chargeth with folly; and we are told that even a juft man falleth feven times a day. In the midft therefore of our exultation we have caufe for humility, and after all to confefs, that not by works of righteoufnefs which we in any way have done doth he fave us, but through his free mercy in Chrift Jefus. And this duly confidered (and whether it be confidered as it ought let us afk our hearts ferioufly) muft raife our

gratitude

gratitude to the higheſt degree; for the due conſideration of it leads on our thoughts to another particular comprehended in our redemption; our having been begotten again thro' God's abundant mercy, unto a lively hope, to an inheritance incorruptible and undefiled that fadeth not away, reſerved in heaven for us.

It is appointed unto all men once to die; now ſetting entirely aſide the thoughts of what may happen to us after death, the very idea of quitting the preſent life is grievous to human nature. To think that the time will ſoon come when we ſhall have no more a portion in any thing that is done under the ſun; when the ſun indeed will riſe but not to ſhine on us; when the uſual buſineſs of the world will be carried on, but with as little regard to us as if we had never been; when the generality of our acquaintance will have intirely forgotten us; and

and thofe whom we now moft love, and who perhaps moft love us, will feldom think of us, or if they do, with almoft perfect indifference; when all that pleafes the eye, charms the ear, and delights the heart, will be withdrawn, and thefe our bodies which we have fo dearly loved and fo carefully fupported, will be laid in the cold and dark grave, there to become a mafs of corruption, from which even our acquaintance and friends would turn afide with averfion—the food of worms. Alas! who can think of thefe things without melancholy dread? Who does not need fome affurances of comfort to fupport his foul under thefe fears of nature? But to imagine further that our very exiftence will ceafe, and our fouls too die with our bodies, carries with it fuch horror as no one could long endure.

God

God therefore has so formed our nature, that tho' we cannot but fear death, we cannot at the same time but hope to live after death, and our reason is capable of furnishing some arguments to encourage this hope of nature; but still, fear will at times prevail in most men, and innumerable difficulties occur to stagger at least if not to silence our reason. The wisest and best of the heathen world are evident instances of this perplexity; at one time they appear convinced, at another full of doubt; at one time supported by proofs, at another embarrassed by objections; one part of man at least, they saw, perished: how necessary this part might be to the enjoyment, if not the existence of the other, who could presume to determine? Besides, tho' they might be convinced of living again after their departure out of this world, yet what is that world into which they were to go? Is it a state of more happiness or more

misery

misery than this? Is it to last longer or shorter than this? Is it to be the final determination of our existence, or are we still to go on thro' successive states? These are questions which reason asks *in vain*: these are apprehensions which *nature suggests*, but reason cannot *dispel*.

Some of these apprehensions of nature we all feel; if we do not feel the rest, we owe this blessing to our early acquaintance with what *he* hath taught us, who hath brought life and immortality to perfect light thro' the gospel; and if we would find a cure for the apprehensions we *do* feel, we have only to acquaint ourselves thoroughly with him and be at peace: he will tell us that the business of this world is only preparatory to more glorious employments hereafter; that its pleasures are not to be compared with those which eye hath not seen nor ear heard; that we are separated

separated from our friends only to meet them again, more amiable and more endearing; that then all our former love will be renewed, heightened, refined, and perfected; that these very bodies which we lay down in the grave shall be restored to us again, exalted and glorious; and, what passes all expression and thought, that we shall be transformed to a state of perfect happiness, no longer subject to diminution, nor to interruption from time or change.

But to whom are we indebted for these invaluable blessings? Innocent creatures can *claim* nothing from God but that their being shall be as good to them as not being, that they shall enjoy as much good as evil: meritorious creatures, were it possible that any creatures could merit from God, can claim nothing further than that their reward shall be proportioned to their merit; but that unprofitable fallen and guilty creatures

tures fhould have any reward, is an act of pure bounty; and that they fhould have fuch a reward as eternal and perfect happinefs, is an act of bounty great beyond all conception. Well therefore is eternal life called in holy fcripture the *gift* of God. Our wages, what we have deferved, is death; but having peace with God thro' our Lord Jefus Chrift, and having accefs by faith into this grace wherein we ftand, we rejoice in hope of the glory of *God*.

ALL this hath Chrift procured for us; all this is he ready to give us in return for a fhort imperfect obedience—peace, light, ftrength, and eternal blifs. And in order to accomplifh this wonderful difpenfation of love, our ever gracious Redeemer, who being in the form of God, thought it not robbery to be equal with God, yet took upon him the form of a fervant, and fubmitted to the loweft offices of human nature;

nature; nay he defcended ftill lower, even to die an ignominious and painful death upon the crofs, becoming himfelf a curfe to redeem us from the curfe of the law, the juft for the unjuft. What a condefcention is this? and how far beyond the power of words to defcribe? Scarcely for a righteous man will one die, yet peradventure for a good man fome would even dare to die; but God commendeth his love to us, in that whilft we were yet finners, Chrift died for us. The eternal Son of God became man, that he might tafte death for all men, and raife them from the depths of mifery and defpair, to the heighth of blifs and heaven. With what grateful joy then ought we to receive thefe gracious proofs of God's goodnefs and mercy, and how earneft fhould we be to fhow forth our gratitude by every act of praife and thankful obedience?

IF

If we drew our being, and derive every thing around us from his all creating hand: if that being be fupported and every comfort and neceffary of life be fupplied by his fatherly providence; is it poffible that we can live in neglect of him, and what is worfe, that we can live in wilful difobedience to his commands: but if we can forget that power and goodnefs which created and preferves us, furely we cannot forget that mercy which hath redeemed us; miferable finners, confcious of guilt and fearing punifhment, cannot forget that love which offers them pardon. Ignorant creatures, confcious of their blindnefs, and walking in darknefs, cannot forget that light which lighteth every man that cometh into the world: frail creatures, confcious of weaknefs, and fearing the dangers which furround them, cannot forget that interceffion which procures them ftrength: unprofitable and perifhing creatures, confcious of their defects, and fearing death, cannot forget thofe merits which have gained them eternal life. Thus might we fairly reafon, did not fad experience prove the contrary: did we not fee men who cannot only forget God, but ufe that Being which he hath given them to counteract his gracious defigns; who can abufe every bleffing his providence affords, and who can even tread under foot the Son of God; count the blood of that covenant, wherewith he was fanctified, an unholy thing; and do defpite unto the fpirit of grace: but God forbid that this fhould be true of any of us! May God give us fuch a fenfe of all his mercies, that our hearts may be unfeignedly thankful, and that we may fhew forth his praife, not only with our lips, but in our lives, by giving up ourfelves to his fervice, and by walking before him in holinefs and righteoufnefs all the days of our life, thro' Jefus Chrift our Lord.

SERMON

SERMON VIII.

Heb. *Ch.* xiii. *V.* 7.

"WHOSE FAITH FOLLOW."

THE faith which the Hebrews were required to follow was the faith of the first preachers and professors of christianity. And if it was incumbent upon them to follow this faith, it is incumbent also upon us; for the same reasons necessarily apply to both. But neither did the Apostle require from his converts a blind acquiescence in the religion he taught, nor do the present preachers of christianity seek to be "Lords over your faith." It is our practice, as it was his, fairly to propose to our hearers the grounds of our religion, addressing ourselves to their understandings, and requiring them to judge for themselves of the reasonableness and obligation of what we advance.

I will endeavor therefore at present to state to you, as briefly and plainly as I can, the obligation and the reasonableness of our believing and practising the christian religion.

On surveying ourselves and the world in which we are placed, we discover every where evident marks of the highest wisdom, power, and goodness. If we inquire how and whence we and the things about us came to be, and trace back to its source this wonderful order and regularity, we are led by the most easy and obvious steps to the acknowledgement of a supreme Being,

the

the firſt great cauſe of all things, who gave exiſtence to us and the whole creation. And as this Being muſt neceſſarily be endued with all perfection, he cannot be regardleſs of his own productions, ſince this would argue variableneſs of will, or want of power, both which are inconſiſtent with the very notion of perfection. From the relation which we bear to him as his creatures, as objects of his conſtant care and inſpection, and experiencing continual inſtances of his favour and goodneſs, we ſurely feel ourſelves obliged to act conformably to his will, in what way ſoever it may have been declared to us. What his will is, our reaſon in ſome reſpects informs us, by clear deductions from his nature and attributes. As he is our Creator and Lord, it plainly becomes us to reverence and adore him: as he has been and is kind and good to us, and has given us affections towards our fellow creatures, the inference is obvious,

vious, that we should exercise those affections and be kind and good to others. And since he is a Being of purity and holiness, and hath endued us with powers capable of resembling him, and formed us for higher enjoyments than any which this world affords, it must surely be our duty as well as happiness to keep the inferior part of our nature in due subordination to the superior, and to strive to imitate him as much as possible in all spiritual improvements.

If moreover these things are thus reasonable and proper, we cannot but infer that the observance of them is required of us; and if we do not observe them, that some time or other, an infinitely holy and just Being will punish us for our neglect, as indeed our consciences, which confirm these deductions of our reason, will, if consulted, and frequently, whether consulted or not, abundantly testify: on the other hand,

hand, if there be a God who thus delights in piety and goodnefs, we muft conclude that there will be fome future ftate in which they will receive more evident marks of his approbation and favor, than thofe which attend them in this life. So far our reafon might go on clear and obvious grounds, and fuch are the difcoveries which it might fatisfactiorily make, in addition to the conclufions, deducible from the more abftrufe and refined fpeculations on the nature and fpirituality of God and of the human foul, on the abftract difference of good and evil, and the natural fitnefs and beauty of the one, and unfitnefs and deformity of the other. But ftill we fhould be left in the dark with refpect to many particulars, and in doubt, at the beft, about many more, which renders us fenfible of our ftanding in need of fome fuperior information. Accordingly we are taught to believe that there hath been an exprefs revelation of the will

will of our Creator; by which all the before mentioned truths are fully confirmed, and in many respects enlarged; many difficulties attending them are accounted for and removed; we are made acquainted with various important articles in which our happiness is deeply concerned, which we could not know before; and we find the belief of what it teaches and the practice of what it commands enforced, amidst other inferior motives, by no less than the promise of eternal happiness and the threatening of eternal misery. What pretends to so high a character as the revealed will of the Almighty, and claims attention upon such interesting motives, cannot be left unnoticed, without wilful disprespect to him and disregard of our real good; for this would be presuming either that he is not able to give us any instructions, tho' we are able to instruct one another, or that we have no need of any: the latter favours of arrogance and

and felf-fufficiency, inconfiftent with our condition; and the former is denying to God all intercourfe with his creatures, and impioufly prefcribing bounds to his infinite wifdom and power. And not to examine that upon which our happinefs both here and hereafter is affirmed to be, and at leaft it is poffible that it may be, dependent, is furely the greateft infatuation.

As this revelation profeffes to addrefs itfelf to the underftandings as well as the hearts of men, accordingly the proofs on which its claims are founded are adapted to reafonable creatures, capable of thinking and acting for themfelves. They are not abfolute demonftrations, for this would have left no power of diffent; and confequently an affent could not be, what from the nature of man it was neceffary that it fhould be, an act of virtue: neither do they when humbly and fairly confidered fall far
fhort

short of demonstration: indeed when collected and considered together, they afford such evidence as no unprejudiced mind can withstand, and fully as much as the nature of the thing can admit.

The most particular and seemingly contradictory prophecies, literally fulfilled in one person several hundred years after they were written, and many of them constantly interpreted of the Messiah, by that very people who rejected his authority and their own interpretations, when he came and fulfilled them: the most astonishing miracles confessed by his very enemies to exceed all human power: the spotless life and *peculiar* character of their author; a character above all former comprehension of men, and consequently incapable of being feigned, and directly contrary to what the known prejudices either of Jews or Gentiles would have led them to feign, had they attempted it:

the

the barbarous treatment, and the painful and ignominious death which he voluntarily underwent to bear witneſs to the truth and ſincerity of his pretenſions: his reſurrection from the grave, evidenced by an intercourſe of forty days with his diſciples, and his appearance to no leſs than five hundred perſons at one time, and his viſible and glorious aſcenſion into heaven: his apoſtles' integrity and extraordinary firmneſs: the power confered upon them by him of knowing the thoughts of mens' hearts, of foretelling future events, of ſpeaking languages which they had never learnt, and of working the greateſt miracles: the teſtimony given by their deaths, and by thoſe of an amazing number of converts of both ſexes and every condition, to the truth of their own and of their maſter's doctrine: the purity, holineſs, and excellence of that doctrine, above the moſt applauded ſyſtems of the moſt learned philoſophers, ſo well adapted to the condition

dition and circumstances of man, exalting his nature, and conducting him to happiness both in this world and the next: and lastly, besides the extraordinary fate of its chief opposers the Jews, and their uncommon dispersion and singular discrimination among all the nations of the earth for more than one thousand seven hundred years; the propagation of this religion in almost every country, tho' in direct contradiction to the most favorite opinions and practices of mankind; and tho' preached at first by a few persons poor and illiterate, and chosen from the lowest occupations, and strenuously opposed by all the power, wealth and learning of the world.

All these things fairly considered, and they are within the comprehension of the most uncultivated minds, cannot fail of producing the fullest conviction: for the objections which from time to time have been made to the nature or circumstances

of

of the evidence are such, as, if admitted, would involve all our knowledge in doubt, and render the world one continued scene of confusion: those which have been made either to the whole dispensation or to some of its parts, are such as were to be expected, from the nature of man and the subject of the dispensation; man being a free agent and capable of error, and the gospel treating of the nature of God and of his universal scheme of providence. Besides this, the pride and vanity of mens' minds, and the corruption of their hearts continually prompt them to transgress such pure and holy laws, and render them unwilling to confess their ignorance and guilt.

That such things would happen, the all wise author of the christian religion foresaw, and very precisely foretold in several parts of the new testament: their happening therefore in conformity with his predictions, must be considered as a confirmation of his authority: but admitting the force of all this, and supposing these things to be true, how and on what evidence, it may be asked, shall we be convinced that they are so? Some of them are established facts open and apparent to every eye: and our belief of the others we may fairly rest on the authority of the holy scriptures, which the following, amidst other arguments, fix on the most solid grounds of credibility.

If the holy scriptures were written at the time and by the persons they are asserted to have been, as the writers had the fullest opportunity of knowing the reality of the facts which they record, and those of the new testament especially were under no imaginable temptation to publish them, nay had every inducement to conceal them, if they had not thought them true; we cannot consistently with our manner of acting

ting in all other ſerious concerns avoid acquieſcing in their teſtimony. And that they were ſo written, is evinced by our enemies the Jews, who maintain the authority of one part of them, which is alſo confirmed by, and ſtrengthens the credibility of the other. They are indeed ſupported by all the evidence that can eſtabliſh the credit of any writings, and abundantly more than any other, which are univerſally received, and whoſe authenticity has never been queſtioned. They were no ſooner written, than copies of them were taken and diſperſed throughout the ſeveral churches, and they were quoted and appealed to in the various controverſies which aroſe in the early times of chriſtianity both with friends and foes. It may be obſerved alſo, that not a few of the facts which they contain are ſupported by the concurrent teſtimony of heathen authors. And if any of them had been falſe, there were not wanting enemies, who eafily could, and with tranfport would have detected and expofed their falfehood, and at once have precluded the facred records from that glorious triumph, which they afterwards obtained, from the numberlefs perfons of all ages and countries, who, with an unexampled conftancy, bore atteftation to the truth and value of them with their lives. In fhort, fo ftrong and fecure is the evidence, on which the authority of the holy fcriptures is founded, that amidft the daring attacks with which the chriftian religion hath been affaulted in every form which malice and ingenuity could fuggeft, few have been the attempts made to overthrow that evidence, though the fuccefs of fuch an effort muft have enfured the fall of the whole fyftem, and without which all other attacks could make but little impreffion.

THE

The bible being thus firmly established as the revelation of God, it follows that it is incumbent upon all, without exception, to whom it is made known, first, to examine with care, and then to believe with reverence, and to practise with sincerity whatever it requires. Limited as our faculties are, we cannot wonder that in a revelation given by infinite wisdom there should be some things which exceed our reason, which, however, since they do not, when rightly considered, contradict it, we are bound upon such a testimony to receive as implicitly, and believe as firmly, as we do those truths which our reason is competent to understand.

And since the Almighty created us at first, and supports us continually, and thus has an absolute right to our obedience, he might with perfect justice have prescribed to us any commands within our power to perform

perform, And we could not have reason to complain of any want of goodness, whatever had been the conditions of obtaining his favor, since he has proposed to us no less a recompence than eternal happiness, and promised us such assistance as will enable us to attain it. Infinite wisdom and goodness certainly would not have established the christian dispensation, if it had not been proper and necessary for mankind. But since God has thought fit to establish it, he undoubtedly requires our compliance with it; and according to his constant denunciations, will resent and punish, as a most affronting indignity, our neglect of it.

ABSOLUTE universal obedience to God in all respects, *i. e.* a total surrender to our Creator of our understandings, our hearts, and our lives, is what both scripture and reason dictate—doctrines the most unconnected with the present state of things, and apparently

apparently of little importance, if delivered on his authority, ought ever to command our refpect, and may have confequences attending them, of which we are not aware. And we know not what we do, when we prefume to reject any thing which he hath taught, or difregard any thing which he hath commanded: only this we know, that in both inftances, he that wilfully infringes a part of the law, is confidered as a tranfgreffor of the whole; and forfeits his title to all the benefits of the chriftian difpenfation. But are no allowances to be made for human frailty and the practice of the world: and muft we entirely refign all power of judging for ourfelves?

For frailty, moft undoubtedly, much allowance will be made, otherwife what will become of the beft of men? But not for wilful tranfgreffion perfifted in without penitence and amendment: nor indeed have
we

we any reaſon to expect allowance for ſuch frailties as we do not ſincerely endeavor to overcome whenever we are ſenſible of them. For it is our duty and our happineſs, to make the improvement of our nature in all its parts, the leading object of our lives. All ſins which we repent of and forſake, and all failings, which as far as we know them, we pray againſt and faithfully ſtrive to ſubdue, the goſpel aſſures us, that for the merits of Chriſts death, God will not remember to our condemnation: but if the wilful obſtinate perſevering offender, *i. e.* the rejecter of his Maker's deſign to render him happy, could finally eſcape; what diſhonour would this reflect on the juſtice and ſovereignty of God. Happy would it be for thoſe perſons, who ſeek to obtain the rewards of duty, in other ways than thoſe which he has pointed out; if they would conſider this, and conform with reverence to the declarations of him, who is truth itſelf,

itself, and in whose purposes there is no variableness, nor shadow of turning!

Where the practice of the world does not interfere with God's commands, it is the part of a truly wise and good man to pay it due attention; but where it does, there can be no doubt whether we ought to obey God or man: and holy scripture strongly cautions us against following a multitude to do evil. Unnecessary singularity is no part of a christian's character; nay, he makes it a point of duty, to conform to other men as far as he innocently and safely can, that he may, with a better grace, and consequently with greater influence of example, differ where he finds it necessary.

As to the liberty of judging for ourselves, that is by no means designed to be taken away or even restrained by the gospel, except

cept in cafes of which we are not competent to judge; nay, we are required to exercife our judgements and to prove all things; only we are to take all circumftances into confideration, with a fair intention of holding faft that which fhall appear to be good. But further it will be urged by fome, and it will be thought by many, that fuch circumfpection and care as all this requires, would take up a large fhare of their time, would lay them under confiderable reftraints, and interfere with the eftablifhed courfe of the bufinefs and amufements of life. The proper anfwer for a minifter of Chrift to make to thefe objections is, to afk—are thefe things required by God or not?—Search the fcriptures and fee: if they be, are you willing to efcape eternal mifery and obtain eternal happinefs upon the terms which infinite wifdom and goodnefs hath thought fit to propofe? What can be more unreafonable

or

or inconsistent, than for men to take so much thought and pains, to encounter so many and grievous discomforts, to subject their darling inclinations to the severest restraints, forego all amusement, and neglect their most pressing concerns, as we frequently see they do, in order to obtain some favorite object, which (rate the things of this world at the highest,) must necessarily be given up in a few years, perhaps to-morrow, or in guarding against the transitory evils of this life; and yet to grudge the small portion of time and pains which is necessary to deliver us from eternal suffering, and secure to us that perfect happiness which is to last for ever?

Not that in reality we take from our engagements here, what we lay out in the purchase of eternal happiness hereafter. This world and the next are parts of the same constitution of things, and that temper and

and conduct which qualify us for heaven, best promote our true interests on earth; that reverential, yet chearful reliance upon the wisdom, goodness, and power of the Father of the universe, that unbounded benevolence and unwearied beneficence, that purity of soul, and that enjoyment of intellectual pleasure, which springs from exalted affections and an enlarged view of things; as they prevent a thousand sources of misery, so do they also constitute in themselves the most delightful of human satisfactions, they expand the heart and give an inexpressible relish to every inferior gratification.

But it was never intended that men should retain their corrupt inclinations, and encourage those views of happiness, whether founded in pleasure or advancement, on which worldly men act, whilst they endeavor to conform outwardly to the commands

mands of the gospel, acting under continual restraint, and suffering perpetual disappointment: but that they should correct their evil propensities by judicious self-government, and embrace those views of happiness, which the word of God proposes, in conformity with the real condition of things, and the whole constitution of human nature; thus actually believing and even feeling that their interest and their happiness are to be found in those paths alone to which their duty leads; and that the Creator *knows, and has ordered what is most for the good of his creatures.*

TRUTH has nothing to fear from the severest investigation; and therefore the advocates for the gospel do not even wish to conceal that there may be some seeming exceptions to this comfortable representation of the effects of christianity: not to dwell on the case of the first professors of it,

who

who were called to extraordinary trials, but who had also, let it be remembered, extraordinary comforts and support: in the present times men may suffer some inconveniencies of different sorts from their strict adherence to the straight path of duty and uniform profession of christian principles; for instance, the loss of some methods of advancing themselves in the world, which persons less conscientious embrace, and also in an irreligious age they may bear the scorn and perhaps the ridicule of those who see not, or will not profess that they see, the grounds upon which they have formed their scheme of conduct: as to the former of these instances, let men only wait and observe the usual result of such practices, (I mean) with respect to *real enjoyment*, which, and not merely what may be accounted the *means* of it, a wise man makes his object of pursuit: and as to the latter instance, time will soon do justice to the character of an
uniform

uniform chriftian, provided it be not diftorted or rendered abfurd by enthufiafm or fuperftition, and thofe very perfons, whofe depraved habits will not permit them to imitate him, will at leaft efteem and reverence, and fometimes even applaud him: and the regard of good men, and the unalloyed approbation of his own confcience, and the confidence of his mafter's favor, will more than make him amends for enduring, if that fhould be his lot, the fcorn of the foolifh and the profligate: but further exceptions to the eafe, the comforts, and the happinefs, which are alledged to flow from chriftian principles, and thofe of greater weight, may be thought to arife from the difficulties which many perfons have to ftruggle with in bringing their temper and difpofition to evangelical habits of duty; and from the great depreffions of fpirits, which fome, even good men, frequently experience, from a fenfe of their failings

failings and infirmities, with the difficulties of *obedience*, contrast the feelings and circumstances which attend *disobedience*.

And are there no difficulties which spring from vicious indulgencies. Can we conceive any thing more grievous and afflicting than the torment of inordinate passions, the strength and violence of which is continually increasing, whilst the powers of gratification are continually lessening? The unpleasantness of restraint, decreases with every act of self-denial; the desire of forbidden gratification, increases with every act of indulgence. If vicious and worldly men have not the labor of restraining their appetites and inclinations, they must be subject to the most wretched of all tyranny, that which springs from indulging them. As to persons of the other description, they have abundant reason for self-satisfaction and comfort; but some of those infirmities,

to

to which human nature is ever liable, in this state of imperfection, prevent their enjoyment of them. The dejection and melancholy, which we sometimes meet with in good persons, arise in a great measure from some bodily disorder, which is to be removed only by proper medical applications; and it would discover itself in some other way, if religion, with which it hath no real connection, did not exist in the world. They may also in some measure be occasioned by mistaken and contracted notions of the nature of religion, by viewing her under the gloomy and distorted aspect of terror and vengeance, instead of contemplating her in her bright and genuine features of mercy and kindness. But this forms no just exception against the benign and animating spirit of true religion: it only proves, that the greatest of all blessings, that heaven ever bestowed on man as well as those which are inferior, is liable to miftake and abufe in the hands of fuch imperfect creatures. And this alfo is an infirmity like the others that have been mentioned, capable of being corrected, or at leaft capable of being prevented by proper difcipline and more enlarged information. But let the fenfualift and the worldling recollect, that if the gloom which is fometimes fpread over the minds of the beft of men, fhould continue unbroken by any gleam of comfort to the lateft evening of their lives, and their fun fhould even fet in clouds, quickly fhall they behold it rifing again in the morn of eternal life, to fhine with unfpotted and undiminifhing fplendour.

Such then are the foundations of that faith which we are required to follow: fuch the obligation and inducements to follow it. It is not a cunningly devifed fable which we are required to follow, but a religion
fupported

supported by facts, testified unto us by those who were eye witnesses of the majesty of our Lord Jesus Christ. It is not a religion full of melancholy and unnecessary self-denial and abstraction from the world; but it is the source of comfort and delight, securing to us the best enjoyment of the nature which God has given us, and conducting us with safety through the dangers of life. It is only *offered* to our choice, not *forced* upon us, because we are free agents and must be in some measure the framers of our own happiness: but we must remember, that, if it be true, to reject or disregard it, through pride, through indolence, through obstinacy, through false shame, through a love of sinful indulgence and attachment to the world, is, *death*; to embrace and hold it fast, *life* eternal.

SERMON IX.

Acts, Ch. i. *V.* 21, 22.

" WHEREFORE, OF THESE MEN, WHICH HAVE ACCOMPANIED WITH US ALL THE TIME THAT THE LORD JESUS WENT IN AND OUT AMONGST US, BEGINNING FROM THE BAPTISM OF JOHN, UNTO THAT SAME DAY WHEN HE WAS TAKEN UP FROM US, MUST ONE BE ORDAINED TO BE A WITNESS, WITH US, OF HIS RESURRECTION."

IF Christ be not risen, (says St. Paul in that beautiful and pathetic exhortation, towards the close of his first epistle to the Corinthians,) then is our preaching vain, and your faith is also vain. On the truth of this fact the importance of every other

recorded

recorded in the gospels, and even the existence of the christian religion must depend. It will therefore be no unsuitable employment of our thoughts, on a day set apart by the church to commemorate a person, who was elected into the number of the Apostles, expressly because he was an unimpeachable witness of this great event, to consider those evidences which render it, at this remote period, to the most scrupulous inquirers, an object of rational belief.

That the scriptures of the new testament were written by the persons whose names they bear; that these persons lived in Judea, and at the time when the events which make the subject of their several histories took place, that they all of them were the Disciples and constant companions of Christ during his ministry upon earth, or derived their information immediately from those thofe who were fo; that their accounts were publifhed on the fpot, in the midft of adverfaries, who had all the authority of the ftate on their fide, who were inftigated by political jealoufies and by religious zeal, and even pledged by the atrocioufnefs of the crime they had committed to difprove them, if it were poffible: thefe are facts, concerning which it will be fufficient to obferve, that the external evidence in fupport of them is fuch, that, if it can be overthrown, the foundation upon which the belief of every diftant tranfaction refts will be overthrown at the fame time, befides that the fcriptures afford a much ftronger internal proof of their own authenticity than any other antient writings can boaft.

That Chrift really died upon the crofs is a fact which has never been difputed, and which indeed could never have been afferted, asserted, if it had not been true. The Evangelists affirm that many persons saw him, conversed with him, and felt him after he was risen from the dead. In this, as in other instances, that which the Apostles had heard, that which they had seen with their eyes, which they had looked on, and which their hands had handled of the word of life, they declared unto the world in their writings and discourses. It has been remarked, that in the different gospels there is some diversity in the circumstances with which the resurrection of our Lord is said to have been accompanied; but it has also been repeatedly and satisfactorily shewn, that in this diversity there is no inconsistence; and that it is no greater than may always be expected in relations of the same event, written, without any preconcerted plan, by different persons, at different intervals of time,

and

and addressed to readers of different descriptions.

To recite the instances of Christ's appearance after his resurrection which are recorded in scripture is unnecessary, because they are so generally known: to enter into a detail of the methods by which judicious critics have reconciled the seeming variations in the accounts of it would lead us too far from the principal object of our consideration. Assuming then, on the credit of what has been said, that the Apostles and first Christians were the authors of the books contained in the new testament, and that there is no inconsistency in them; but without insisting on their authority as inspired writings; we can have but two reasons against admitting the testimony they contain; either that the Evangelists were themselves deceived, or that they intended to deceive others; that they

were

were not competent, or not faithful witnesses of the fact. For, as to those who deny to God the power of raising a dead person to life, while yet they allow that he created man in the beginning, or who deny that he created man at all, they are not concerned in this argument; they have much to unlearn before they can be admitted to the examination of it.

First then, it must be remembered, that it is affirmed, not that our Lord appeared once, or at a particular hour of the night, or to any one person, or always to the same persons; but that he appeared frequently, during forty days together, at different hours, in the day as well as in the night, to several persons, and to different persons at different times. However, we may imagine, that one or two of the followers of Christ, deeply affected by the circumstances of his death, musing on the probable

probable import of some of his expressions, and assisted in their enthusiasm by concomitant circumstances of solitude, silence, and obscurity, might, immediately after his crucifixion, have suffered themselves to be deluded by the visions of their fancy; it can never be seriously asserted that so great a number of them as saw him on the third day after his death should all be imposed on; it is absolutely impossible that they should continue to be so, with all the means of examination which were afforded them during so long a period. It is related that they saw him eat, that they touched his hands and his feet, that he conversed with them on various subjects, expounding the scriptures to them, and giving them directions for their conduct. Could they be mistaken in all this? If they could, this world affords nothing for belief to rest on.

Nor

Nor must it be forgotten, that the minds of the disciples were in a state by no means fit to contribute to such an illusion; they had always been slow of apprehension and belief, and had now given up all the hopes they had fondly conceived from misinterpreted predictions, and from the supernatural powers they had seen displayed by their Lord. We thought, said two of them, it had been he who should have restored the kingdom to Israel. But, with his life ended every expectation of temporal grandeur, the only expectation they appear to have formed previous to his resurrection, or perhaps to his ascension. In this disposition they were more likely to err on the side of caution than of credulity: we find accordingly, that the two disciples who have been mentioned, though they had heard the testimony of the women, who affirmed that they had seen a vision of angels, which said that Jesus was alive; though several of their

their own company had been eye witnesses that the circumstances of the sepulchre corresponded with this report; though in confirmation of it, the prophecies relating to the Messiah, from Moses downwards, had been explained to them, in a manner which they felt to be something extraordinary, while their hearts burned within them; yet do not appear to have been convinced till their eyes were opened, and he became known to them in the breaking of bread. The minds of the apostles themselves were in the same state; the words of the women appeared to them as idle tales; they doubted and wondered, till their assent was extorted by the fullest and most irrefragable proofs, insomuch that Jesus upbraided them with their unbelief, and the hardness of their hearts.

As little can it be supposed that they were mistaken respecting the supernatural powers

powers with which they affirm that they were invested in confequence of their Lord's refurrection and afcenfion. A number of men, who, on a variety of trying occafions, maintained fo calm and prudent a conduct as the apoftles did; who taught a doctrine fo reafonable, fo free from every tincture of enthufiafm; could never have believed that they wrought miracles of the moft unqueftionable kind, and converfed in languages they had never learned, while in reality they poffeffed no fuch powers. There is therefore no pretence for faying that the writers of the new teftament were deceived themfelves; if their narrations are untrue, it was their intention to deceive others.

Now, in the firft place, fuppofing that our Saviour was holden under the power of death, as other men are, it was very unlikely that his followers fhould make any

any attempt towards supporting his credit. Convinced, as they must have been, that he was an impostor, in his pretences to the office of the Messiah, they were more likely to be indignant at the deception he had put on them, and at the disappointment of their hopes, than to engage in any new undertaking to carry on a design which had received so signal and disgraceful a check: or if, suppressing these feelings, they acted on a mere calculation of interest, what was the interest they pursued, what their probability of success; did they propose to themselves honor, or power, or wealth? These, as has been observed, were among the inducements which attached them to their master during his life. Then they were elated with the expectation of sitting on his right hand and on his left in the temporal kingdom to which their eyes were directed; but now the case was altered. Supposing Christ dead

dead to rife no more, all hope of this kind muft die within them; and that all hope did die appears plainly from their conduct. Nay, when during our Lord's continuance on earth after his refurrection, it feemed, fo deeply rooted was it in their hearts, to revive for a time, at his afcenfion it was finally annihilated, or rather the nature of it was changed from carnal to fpiritual, from temporal to eternal; and we hear no more of a kingdom of this world to be reftored to Ifrael.

BESIDES, the Apoftles' tempers and notions were plainly not of that kind which could lead them into a hope of obtaining heaven by what, if it was an impofture, was an impofture of the moft impious kind. But, admitting that their former ambitious views had ftill fuch an afcendency in their minds as to fuperfede every other confideration, could they be fo infatuated as to imagine

imagine that it was by an adherence to the cause of their crucified master that such views could ever be accomplished? Riches, reputation, and power, were engaged on the opposite side, while the only prospect presented to the followers of Jesus, and which was too soon realised, was poverty, affliction, stripes, imprisonment, and death. If their master had fallen a sacrifice to the envy and malice of his own nation, and the suspicious jealousy of the Romans, was it probable that a persecution, in which bigotry and policy were united, would stop at him? If such things had been done in the green tree, what was to be expected in the dry? Or suppose that they could, at first, have encouraged so chimerical a notion, as that, with every circumstance, humanly speaking, against them, they might still be successful; how could they persevere in it after they had begun to experience its fallaciousness; after some of them

had

had been imprifoned and beaten, and one of their number, Saint Stephen, had been put to death before their eyes? Saint Paul, at leaft, could not be under the influence of any preconceived opinions.

Long after the difciples had ceafed to hope that the rewards to be beftowed on them by their mafter were of a temporal kind, he was ftill immerfed in the ftudy, and diftinguifhed among the moft zealous adherents, of the ceremonial law: he even thought it a crime to continue an inactive fpectator of the progrefs of doctrines, which tended to fubvert the religion of his country, and, in the fpirit of a Pharifee, armed himfelf with the civil power, for the purpofe of extirpating them. Yet this man, ardent indeed in his temper, but untinctured with fanaticifm; and, as both his writings and his conduct teftify, fedate and fober in his judgement; was induced to feparate himself from the party to which he had always been attached by principle, affection, and interest, to renounce a religion which he knew to have been divinely established, and had been used to consider as of eternal obligation; to glory in the cross of Christ, and to count all that he had forfeited as dross, compared with that crown of glory to be received by the faithful at the resurrection of the dead. No less a cause than that assigned in scripture, can be conceived to have produced such a change; but if that cause be admitted, it is in itself decisive of the subject we are considering.

Let it however be supposed, (for this is a case in which the most extravagant suppositions have been made,) that the apostles had some unknown inexplicable motive for wishing to deceive their contemporaries and posterity. Was there the least probability of success to encourage them to make

the

the attempt? Or if enthufiafm rendered them blind to every obftacle, their blindnefs might have proved fatal to themfelves, but would it have effected their purpofe? While the corpfe of their mafter remained in the poffeffion of the adverfe party, all pretences of a refurrection might be inftantly confuted by the mere production of it. It was abfolutely neceffary that they fhould get it into their hands, and within the time which, as was well known to the priefts and Pharifees, he had prefixed for his rifing again. But the fepulcre was fealed, and watched by a guard whom it was not eafy to overpower by force; befides that force, could it have prevailed, would have defeated its own end, and whofe vigilance it was impoffible to elude. The idle tale of the body having been ftolen, while a number of foldiers, trained in the Roman difcipline, were all afleep, was calculated only for the vulgar, and is the ftrongeft confirmation

confirmation of the fact it was intended to difcredit.

Even if we go one ftep farther, and admit, not only that fuch an attempt was made without any reafonable inducement, but that it fucceeded by fome unaccountable means; ftill a material difficulty remains. Perfons who invent or abet a falfehood for fordid ends, recant with as little fcruple when called on by intereft to do fo. We know with what avidity fuch a recantation would have been received, how liberally it would have been rewarded, how induftrioufly it would have been propagated by the rulers of the Jewifh nation: yet, after twenty years had elapfed, a period more than fufficient to extinguifh every hope of temporal advantages, though of five hundred brethren, who had feen our Saviour at once after his refurrection, the greater part was ftill alive; not one, in fo

great

great a number was found to faulter in his teftimony, and many of them, after perfevering in it calmly through life, amidft every difcouragement and affliction, fealed it at laft in their blood.

Why it pleafed our bleffed Lord to fhew himfelf to thefe chofen witneffes, and not to all the people, it would be of no confequence to the validity of their teftimony whether we could difcover or not. Convincing reafons have, however, been affigned by able and difpaffionate inquirers; for, I had almoft faid, the neceffity of fuch a felection.

The fact of Chrift's refurrection is fo intimately connected with every other fact and doctrine contained in the new teftament, that it's truth, once eftablifhed, implies the truth of the reft. They are, however, capable of an independent proof, and from

from arguments exactly similar to those which have been adduced. In their reports of their master's miracles and discourses, the apostles had no inducement to deceive others, they could not be deceived themselves.

It is not possible to see, without equal surprise and concern, persons professing to be employed in the search of truth, and yet from prejudice, or the affectation of singularity, resisting such accumulated evidence, and rejecting a religion which alone affords a foundation of reasonable hope, consistent principles, and uniform conduct.

SERMON

SERMON X.

DEUTERONOMY, *Ch.* xxix. *V.* 29.

"THE SECRET THINGS BELONG UNTO THE LORD OUR GOD; BUT THOSE THINGS WHICH ARE REVEALED BELONG UNTO US AND OUR CHILDREN FOR EVER, THAT WE MAY DO ALL THE WORDS OF THIS LAW."

THE more attention we pay to the conduct of mankind, the more we shall be convinced of the truth of an old observation; that nothing is a greater proof of sound judgement than the avoiding all extremes; and yet, few are to be found who steadily maintain that middle course which leads to the attainment of happiness, and to the degree of perfection in virtue, and science, of which human nature is capable. Instances are perpetually forcing themselves on our notice in the ordinary transactions of life; and, if we direct our view to (what may be considered as a superior department) the conduct of the understanding, by men who profess to exercise thought and reflection; we shall see abilities, that might have been successfully employed in the search of truth, prevented and rendered useless by presumption, scepticism, or refinement.

MANY there are so confident of their abilities, as to persuade themselves that they are capable of penetrating the inmost recesses of nature, and the most mysterious dispensations of providence. Accordingly, whatever they cannot comprehend is pronounced to have no existence; whatever they suppose they have discovered, how-

ever

ever subtle and abstruse, however contradictory to the general sense of mankind, is affirmed with the most dogmatical assurance. On the other hand, there are persons, who, because some things are inscrutable, and many things admit only a partial investigation, consider the pursuit of truth as the pursuit of a chimæra, and give themselves up to universal scepticism, or sink into intellectual indolence. Antient philosophy furnishes examples of both these dangerous extremes; and would that modern philosophy, would that modern theology did not! The words of the text contain a concise direction by which they may both be avoided. They suggest that there are some things which concern God only, and which man will in vain attempt to discover; but that others, in which also God is concerned, it is not only allowable, but absolutely incumbent on man to investigate, since the performance of the duty he

owes

owes to his creator will depend, in no small degree, on his forming just conceptions of them.

A consideration of these two propositions, will comprehend the case of natural, as well as of revealed religion. First, the secret things belong unto the Lord our God.

When, after having made provision for the absolute necessaries of life, the active mind of man began to find leisure for reflection; no speculation would appear so interesting and important, as an inquiry into his own origin, into the purpose and tendency of his present state of existence. Reason, in this, as in other subjects, proceeding from what is obvious and sensible, to what is remote and abstruse, would gradually ascend from the visible things of this world to the invisible things of him who made them; and having collected, with a

certain

certain degree of evidence and precision, the being and attributes of God, would infer from them his moral government, and the probability of future retribution.

The wifest of the antient philosophers, without any biafs from prejudice on his mind; (for he knew not that any authentic revelation exifted, or had ever been promifed to mankind) confidered it however as no improbable event, that conclufions, fo formed, might in due time be confirmed or corrected by immediate communications from heaven; that others might be fuggefted, which, though perhaps difcoverable by reafon in the procefs of inquiry, had not been actually difcovered; and farther, that certain peculiarities of the divine nature might alfo be imparted, together with duties and confequences refulting from them, which, not being deducible from any facts or principles previoufly known, would reft

folely

solely on the authority by which they were revealed.

Those who reject revelation on the ground of its being superfluous, do not, it is presumed, rate the powers of the human understanding so highly, as to imagine that no limits are assigned to its progress: every hour's experience too sensibly confutes any such pretension. The subjects with which men are continually conversant, and which they have means of submitting to the most rigorous examination, are yet but superficially known. There is something that so completely baffles all researches, pursued beyond a certain point, as even to preclude conjecture. And shall that intellect, which forms only confused ideas of its own functions, and of the material frame to which it is united, be thought capable of comprehending the universal system, and of fathoming the purposes of omnipotence? But, if the

the affertion means only that whatever is neceffary to be known may be difcovered without fupernatural affiftance, and that confequently no fuch affiftance has been given; this implies that there are alfo fecret things belonging to God, with which it is not neceffary that man, in his prefent ftate at leaft, fhould be acquainted.

On the other hand, to admit that a revelation has been given, is tacitly to acknowledge the natural infufficiency of the human faculties; all unneceffary interpofitions being fo contrary to the evident plan of the divine adminiftration, that the objection of thofe who deny the authenticity of fcripture on this ground can only be fet afide, by fhewing that the affertion on which it is founded is untrue.

But the admonition of the text, it may be faid, addreffed to a people who lived
confeffedly

confessedly under a law of types and figures, and beheld, as through a glass, darkly; is not applicable to christians, who see those things which many prophets and righteous men desired to see, and saw them not; whom the day spring from on high hath visited, and on whom the sun of righteousness is risen. The question therefore with believers is, whether that fuller communication of divine truth, which has been vouchsafed to mankind in the new testament, enables them to investigate it in all its circumstances, and to its utmost extent.

The analogy discoverable between the system of nature, and that of revealed religion, has been alleged as a strong presumption that they are derived from the same author. Of the various instances into which this analogy branches, the case under consideration is one. That multiplicity of ingenious inventions, by which society in
its

its prefent improved ftate is furnifhed, not only with the neceffaries, but with the conveniencies and elegancies of life, in fo ample a manner, that imagination can fcarce devife a farther refinement on them, teftifies how gracioufly man's faculties are adapted to explore the properties of matter, fo far as a knowledge of them can contribute to his ufe or enjoyment. The impenetrable obfcurity, in which others of its qualities are enveloped, fhews that no indulgence was intended to what, within his prefent fphere of action, is probably a vain curiofity.

A SIMILAR procedure of providence is obfervable in our fpiritual concerns. This life is a ftate of moral probation, and the proper bufinefs of mankind, during their continuance in it, is to acquire fuch ideas of their relation to God and to each other, and to form fuch habits of action, correfpondent to thefe relations, as may qualify them hereafter for employments of a more exalted kind, and of more extenfive utility. In the profecution of thefe fubjects, they have been affifted, from time to time, by communications from above, fuited to the exigencies of the feveral periods at which they took place. (Why thefe communications were gradual, why they were not more explicit, makes no part of the prefent difcuffion; though, confiftently with that caution and refpect which fhould accompany all attempts to explain the divine œconomy, a rational account of it might be given.) Finally, the Meffiah, in whom all the counfels of God were compleat, appeared in the world, and having promulgated a religion, which in due time was to overfpread the earth, bequeathed to mankind the everlafting Gofpel, the ultimate declaration of the will and gracious purpofes of his Father.

This

This Gospel is styled, by those who transmitted it to posterity, a marvelous light, so radient that those who walk in it are denominated children of light and of the day. And well do those writings deserve the name, which teach authoritatively what is that true, and acceptable, and perfect will of God, comprised in a system of morality founded on the purest principles, and of religious worship, fit for spiritual beings to pay, and for the Father of spirits to receive: which afford such views of the nature and providence of God, as conduce essentially to the promotion of virtue and happiness; the great and inseparable purposes of our being: which, while they confirm the deductions of reason concerning the existence and attributes of the Deity, sooth the mind with displays of his benignity and condescension to the infirmities of his creatures, beyond what they could have presumed to hope, or were able to conceive.

Without the aid of revelation it never could have been known that the appropriate office of a being, partaking of the divine nature, is to fanctify the hearts, and confirm the wavering refolutions of thofe who pioufly and humbly implore his facred influence. That the Son of God, the brightnefs of his Father's glory, by whom alfo he made the world, fhould fo fympathife with the fallen ftate of mankind, as to diveft himfelf of that glory, to become the voluntary inftrument of his Father's mercy, the mediator of a new and better covenant; nay, that he fhould account the benefits which accrue to man from this unexampled felf abafement, a recompence for the hardfhips, and contumely to which his life was expofed, and for the painful and ignominious death by which it was terminated.

No difpenfation could fo ftrikingly have exemplified the price of virtue in the fight of of God, as his sending his only Son into the world to enforce it both by precept and example. Nothing could have afforded such support and encouragement, under every difficulty and calamity to which we may be exposed by an adherence to it, as this illustrious instance, that a state even of severe and long continued suffering, is compatible with the most perfect love and highest approbation of our Governor and Judge. Nothing could more effectually vindicate the mysterious schemes of his providence to men and angels, than the ultimate triumph of oppressed virtue over successful malice; the exaltation of Christ to be a Prince and Saviour, while his enemies were humbled in the dust.

Thus, in the science of religion, as well as in that of nature, all that it imports man to know, has been conveyed to him in the way best adapted to improve his understanding,

ding, and to touch his heart. But, when he would purfue this fubject through all its extent and all its detail, when he engages in abftrufe fpeculations, too well known from the eager difputes and unchriftian animofities, they have excited, to need being enumerated here, all is obfcurity and error. Scripture affords no light, and in no inftance has it been treated with more irreverance, or received greater injury, than in prefumptuous applications of it to fubjects which it never was intended to explain. Senfes and faculties effentially different from thofe which divine wifdom has beftowed on man, as beft fuited to the place he at prefent occupies in the fcale of creation, may be neceffary to the comprehenfion of thofe fubjects refpecting which he bewilders himfelf in vain. A wider field of fpeculation might have detached him too much from thofe practical duties in which fo great a part of his trial confifts. It is not improbable that

that the history of the first pair was in part intended for a warning to their posterity, to stop with reverence at the bounds which are prescribed to human knowledge. Few in depth of thought and research have excelled the great epic poet of this nation, nor was he unconscious of the powers he possessed; yet, as is well known, the pursuit of what he calls vain wisdom and false philosophy, is among the instances he has chosen to exemplify the perverse dispositions of the fallen angels.

Men who had fabricated an imposture for interested purposes, would have had recourse to artifices of conciliation, to compensate the deficiency of truth; and availed themselves of the curiosity so prevalent among Jews and Heathens, by professing to gratify it with authentic communications from heaven. The object of Christ and the Apostles, was not to please the world, but to do the will of him who sent them; they preached the doctrines that were to make men wise unto salvation, and would have held it profane to endeavour to procure them a reception by any other means than their proper evidence.

As the silence of revelation, on points respecting which no information can be derived from any other source, is a proof that they were not intended to be known by man, and ought to repress premature curiosity: so, on the other hand, the very existence of a revelation, duly authenticated, imposes on those to whom it is addressed, the strictest obligation to acquaint themselves, according to the measure of their talents and opportunities, with whatever it contains.

AUTHORS who profess to develope the secret springs of human policy, and to point out but the origin and tendency of tranfactions, which, to an ordinary eye, appear fortuitous and unconnected, are read with avidity, and ftudied with the clofeft attention. Analogies are carefully drawn between the actual ftate of things, and that which is defcribed, and leffons of enterprife or caution are derived from them; fometimes with the more felfifh view of perfonal aggrandifement; fometimes with the nobler one of converting them to the benefit of mankind. But where is the fcience, where the object of purfuit, that gives fuch fcope both to the powers of the underftanding, and the beft emotions of the heart, as a minute and unprejudiced inveftigation of the hiftory of God's dealings with man; from the offence of the firft Adam, in whom we all die, to the advent and miniftry of the fecond, in whom we all are made alive.

THE

The folemnity and awful circumftances, by which this difpenfation has been diftinguifhed through the feveral ftages of its progrefs, are calculated to awaken the moft infenfible, and to fix the attention of the moft unthinking. Experience has fhewn, and we have already had occafion to obferve, that the human faculties, however limited in certain refpects, are adequate to all the concerns of the prefent life; they are in themfelves the fource of intellectual pleafure, an enjoyment of a ftill higher kind; they penetrate the abyfs of fpace, and reduce to order and fyftem objects of which the remotenefs feems to mock inquiry, and the vaftnefs to furpafs a finite comprehenfion.

To the direction of thefe faculties mankind are left in the moft difficult, and in, what appear to them, the moft important and interefting conjectures. Empires rife
and

fall, revolutions take place which convulfe the world, virtue is oppreffed, and vice triumphant: ftill, all appears to proceed according to an eftablifhed order of caufes and effects; no voice is heard from heaven; whatever fhare an overruling power may have in producing or controuling fuch events, its influence is fo filent and indirect, as (even when they come to be difpaffionately ftudied in the page of hiftory, and with a more extended view of their connections and confequences,) to afford rather matter of conjecture than of certainty.

From this plan, fo generally, and, as even our imperfect apprehenfion can difcover, fo wifely adhered to, we find but one deviation, though the records we poffefs are almoft coeval with the exiftence of our race. For, the prophecies, the calling of Abraham, the miraculous communications and deliverances vouchfafed to the
Patriarchs

Patriarchs and their defcendants, the fingular polity of the Jews, all were preparatory and fubordinate to that myftery into which even the angelic hoft were defirous to look; that fecond creation, more glorious than the firft, when the morning ftars fang together, and the fons of God fhouted for joy. Well indeed did the divine purpofe, in fending the Meffiah upon earth, correfpond to thofe awful difplays of fupernatural power by which it was prefigured and accompanied. It was not to adjuft the petty interefts of individuals or ftates, it comprifed not one fleeting generation of men; but, having been decreed in the counfels of God before the foundation of the world, it reached from the beginning to the confummation of all things; conferring on myriads, to whom it never was promulgated, a ftate of blifs, fuch as eye hath not feen, nor ear heard, nor hath it entered into to the heart of man to conceive; incorruptible, eternal in the heavens.

But however benevolent the original purpose of God in the formation of man, however his spirit has since continued to strive with the perversity of his creatures, it appears from the whole tenor of scripture, that a certain degree of co-operation on their part is indispensible to the attainment of the happiness that awaits them; nay, that happiness in a rational being implies, and is inseparable from, the practice and consciousness of virtue. The idea of God's benevolence is not more confirmed by the inestimable benefit of redemption, than the necessity of doing all the words of his law is enforced by the mode in which it was conferred. Instead of pronouncing an unconditional pardon, which perhaps would have been inconsistent with his attributes, he sent Christ upon earth to be at once a

preacher

preacher and example of moral and religious duties. The conduct of the Son of God was invariably regulated by those principles which reason and conscience dictate to mankind, and this strict conformity to them was so far from being derrogatory from the dignity of his nature, that it is assigned as the cause of his exaltation above all principalities and powers, and of his investiture with a kingdom which shall have no end, the sceptre of which is emphatically called a sceptre of righteousness. It is essential that the character of the subjects of this kingdom should resemble that of their Sovereign: to form such a character is a work of care and time. Fitness for the comparatively trifling employments of our present state implies a previous course of instruction, continual application, and much practice: and as the seasons of childhood and youth are seasons of preparation for the duties of maturer age, so the whole of

this

this mortal life is a feason in which principles and habits are to be acquired that may qualify us for the life to come.

In the acquisition of the principles there is no difficulty, or danger of being misled. They are contained in books written by persons divinely commissioned to impart them, and imparted with such plainness and simplicity, that the commonest understanding is competent to discern the great truths necessary to salvation. By frequent meditation on these sacred truths, man becomes impressed with sentiments of love and reverence for the author of all that is good; his views are gradually enlarged, and he learns, not, as some vainly affect, to undervalue the employments and blessings of this transitory state, but to appreciate them by the relation they bear to that to which he aspires. In proportion as the mind is so constituted, the creature approximates,

proximates, vaſt as the interval muſt always be, to a reſemblance of him who made him. What is ſinful, by degrees ceaſes to be a temptation, and becomes an object of abhorrence: what is juſt and holy is no longer a taſk, but the attracting power to which his heart ſeems inſtinctively to turn. There is no unreaſonableneſs in ſuppoſing that admiſſion to a more intimate acquaintance with the perfections of God, and appointments to offices of more important truſt, may conſtitute, to a ſpirit ſo prepared and trained, that ineffable bleſſedneſs reſerved for thoſe who have been faithful in the things committed to them here below. But what remains for thoſe whoſe faculties have been immerſed in ſloth, or brutalized by ſenſual pleaſures? What, at beſt, but the unſatisfied cravings of degenerate appetites, ſince they have rendered themſelves incapable of taſting any happineſs
that

that is fit for a pure and holy being to bestow.

It is not meant to be affirmed that the whole of what is revealed, though it is revealed for our edification, and belongs to us and to our children, is therefore open to the apprehension of every man who may search the scriptures with a serious purpose, and with his best attention. Persons whose understandings, naturally strong, have been improved by culture, and who have leisure for contemplation, will discover, both directly and by inference, what escapes an ordinary reader; but, if they have been actuated in their researches by a motive worthy of the subject, they will consider the diffusion of these discoveries as the best acknowledgement they can make, in their humble sphere, to the Father of lights, from whom all knowledge is derived, and who dispenses his gifts unequally, in order to give fcope to the exercife of benevolence among the members of that body, which is fitly joined and compacted by that which every joint fupplieth, and of which the head is Chrift. An intimate knowledge of hiftory, of the language and opinions, the cuftoms and manners of antiquity, efpecially of the countries which were the fcenes of the principal events recorded in holy writ, joined to an acquaintance with thofe improvements in fcience which God has afforded to thefe later ages, enables men to avail themfelves more and more of that light which fhined fo long in darknefs, while the darknefs comprehended it not; and caufes the fcorn with which feeming inconfiftences have been treated by a fuperficial petulant fect, in modern times mif-named philofophers, to recoil on themfelves.

The rule, laid down in the former part of the text, is not infringed by the most accurate investigation of scripture, nor by fair deductions from what it really contains, but by unauthorised theories, which minister questions, rather than godly edifying; and confident conclusions respecting the ways of providence, the result of crude conceptions, and short sighted views. Those who are desirous to know all the words of the law, in order to do them, proceed step by step, and with reverential caution: it cannot indeed be denied, that persons whose lives and principles, in the main, were truly pious, have sometimes overstepped the boundary prescribed to them, and in this instance betrayed an over weening opinion of themselves, and a fondness for admiration; faults far removed from the genuine spirit of christianity. Let us not, however, be seduced by what is laudable in their conduct, into a participation of their error; but above all, let us beware of the example of thofe who offend in both points; who are fo engroffed by unprofitable fpeculations as to difregard the fubftance of religion, and incur at once the blame of prefumption and neglect.

SERMON

SERMON XI.*

HAGGAI, *Ch.* i. *V.* 5.

"THUS SAITH THE LORD, CONSIDER YOUR WAYS."

WHEN one person desires another only to consider what is most for his real good, and whether he be pursuing it or not, he would be sure, we may presume, of obtaining his request.

WHEN the Almighty, the Creator and Governor of the Universe, who gave mankind their existence, and supports it by his continual favour, condescends to address himself

* Preached in Lent 1794.

himself to them in similar language, it must be the height of obstinacy and perverseness to neglect it; and that it may not be neglected, the church has taken care to have it particularly offered to our attention, by appointing a season for self-recollection.

On considering the nature of man, it is apparent, not only that it is composed of two parts, the one external, which we perceive with our senses, and the other internal, which we discover only by reflection; but that this internal part is likewise made up of various particulars, possessing different degrees of importance, all of which are united together and form a whole, some being evidently in subordination to others. The real happiness therefore of such a being, must arise from keeping each part in due order, that the general constitution of his inward frame may not be injured: he must afford to each particular only such indulgence

dulgence as its rank demands, and fuch as is confiftent with allowing proper regard to every other: he muft gratify his appetite and his paffions in fuch manner and degree, as nct to debafe his affections in difregard of his reafon and his confcience. But a very little acquaintance with human nature, too plainly convinces us that this harmony which fhould arife from the due regulation of the various parts of our internal frame, is in all perfons confiderably difturbed, and in the generality of mankind to fuch a degree, that inftead of acting with an eye to every part of their nature, and principally to the fuperior part, they follow thoughtleffly the impulfe of the loweft, as circumftances accidently determine:

From hence fprings continual difquiet, fimilar to that which is experienced in any civil government when due order and fubordination are deftroyed, aud the inferior members of society usurp the place of the highest. And besides this internal disgust which springs naturally from the destruction of order in our minds, there is a source of uneasiness upon the whole still more distressing which arrives from a sense of guilt, and which must by some means or other be allayed, or our happiness is utterly destroyed. Every one that reflects upon his nature and his condition, and considers them (what they really are) as the appointments of a superior power, must know that he is responsible to that power for not having acted according to that nature, and the motives which he may by any means have received of his maker's will; nay, whether he reflects or not, of this truth, the superior part of his frame, his conscience, will at times render him sufficiently sensible.

When from the nature of man we turn to the contemplation of his external condition

dition in the present world, the first thing likely to strike us, is the mixture of good and evil in the various situations of human life: that as there is no state of suffering (such is the goodness of our heavenly Father) which excludes every source of satisfaction, so there is no state of enjoyment unattended by some disagreeable circumstances. In the early morning of life when all things appear gay and captivating to our imaginations, dressed in the charms of novelty, we are apt to entertain more flattering notions; and if our domestic situation be upon the whole comfortable, as we feel not, from the merciful provisions of providence for the tender years of childhood, the inconveniences of our situation, or at least those only which are short lived, we are led to think that human life may be rendered one continued course of enjoyment; but this delusion gradually retires as we proceed, vanishing altogether, long before our sun has

has attained its meridian height: and, as extremes ever beget one another, this unreasonable expectation of enjoyment too often ends in exceffive fears of the evils of life, and inattention to its real good.

Another thing, which no great experience of human affairs is fufficient to teach a reflecting perfon, is—the natural unfatisfactorinefs of every earthly enjoyment. Things appear to our minds extremely defirable and capable of affording the higheft degree of continued happinefs, which are found after a while to lofe in poffeffion all power of delighting, and to be unable to exclude from our lives infipidity and difguft. Of this all perfons are fenfible as far as their experience has hitherto extended; but moft perfons, looking for the caufe of it not where it really exifts, in the general nature of fublunary objects, but fuppofing it to be in the particular nature of the objects

jects which have engaged their attention with fresh hopes, divert their pursuit to other objects, which are sure to produce fresh disappointment, till at length they too often grow discontented with the world, and repine at the wise and gracious dispensations of providence, and drag out the remainder of their days in peevish dissatisfaction with themselves, and every thing around them.

A THIRD circumstance in our present condition, will unavoidably strike us whether we consider it or not. The most extended age of man, taken in one point of view, is but a lesson of the shortness of human life, and almost every day affords some instance of its uncertainty. This point requires no enlargement; the bare mention of it brings a cloud over the brightest face, and the thoughts of it, which will sometimes occur, can arrest for a time the most eager pursuit purfuit of bufinefs, of ambition, or of pleafure. All flefh is as grafs, and all the glory of man as the flower of grafs; the grafs withereth, and the flower thereof falleth away.

Now, for a being poffeffed of fuch a nature, and placed in fuch circumftances, what is the proper fcheme of life, in order to fecure his greateft good? Certainly one, (if it can be found) which will reftore to their proper order all the parts of his inward frame, and quiet the fears and apprehenfions of guilt; thus procuring peace and ferenity of mind: one which will enable him to take as much of the good things of human life, with as little of the evil as is poffible: one which will teach him how to prolong the power of receiving fatisfaction from the pleafures of it: and laftly, one which will enable him to look with fteadfaft hope beyond the boundaries of the prefent sent contracted state of existence, and to be easy in his mind notwithstanding the uncertainty of it.

And is there not such a scheme of life to be found? Do we not indeed already possess it in that which is pointed out to us by the christian religion? Is it not the professed aim of the christian religion to remedy the evils which spring from the disorder of our internal frame, and by reducing each part to its due state, to restore the original harmony of our minds? Does it not endeavour to restrain our appetites within the bounds proper to the inferior part of our nature, to moderate our passions, to refine and exalt our affections, to enlarge our conceptions, and correct our judgment, to quicken our sense of right and wrong—by precept, by example, by discoveries, by extraordinary assistance? The fears and apprehensions of guilt ought to vanish at once from

from every afflicted breaſt on hearing the aſſurances contained in the goſpel, of the willingneſs of our heavenly Father to receive all ſuch as turn unto him with hearty repentance and true faith in his Son Jeſus Chriſt.—Come unto me, ſaid the Redeemer of the world, all ye that travail and are heavy laden, and I will refreſh you. So God loved the world, that he gave his only begotten Son, to the end that all who believe in him ſhould not periſh but have eternal life. He was ſent to heal the broken hearted, to preach deliverance to the captives, and recovering of ſight to the blind, to ſet at liberty them which are bruiſed, to preach the acceptable year of the Lord.—Acquaint yourſelves then with the merciful Jeſus and be at peace. Though your ſins be red as ſcarlet, they ſhall be made white as ſnow; and though they be as purple, they ſhall be made white as wool.

WITH

With refpect to the mixture of good and evil in the prefent world: evils, which come not unexpected, lofe much of their power, for they bring not with them the bitternefs of difappointment. Now, in what light is the prefent ftate of our exiftence reprefented in the gofpel of Chrift? Is this world any where reprefented as a ftate of perfect eafe, and undifturbed enjoyment? Is it not reprefented juft as we find it, and fuch as we might expect to find a ftate of probationary education, which is to *introduce* us to a ftate of reft and perfect happinefs?

If then we will enter upon the world as chriftian faith will lead us, we fhall enter upon it with the knowledge of its nature, which is ufually derived from experience, accompanied by the advantage of not having our minds depreffed, and our relifh of enjoyment blunted by unhappy difappointment

ment of too sanguine expectations: and we shall also learn how to make the least of the evil and the most of the good. Christianity prevents by the caution which it gives, many particular evils which swell the general load of calamity, and it assuages the anguish of such as are unavoidable, nay, almost alters their nature. Recollect how large a portion of human calamity arises from an ungoverned imagination, and vain fears and anxieties about future events; how much of it springs from vicious indulgences, and wrong or hard hearted conduct of one sort or another: and then consider what a check to all these evils is provided by the christian religion? For one part, in that just, sober, enlarged view of things, suggested by contemplating the œconomy of the gospel dispensation, and by a thorough belief that all *events* are under the direction of infinite wisdom, goodness, and power.—For the other part, in the

the prevalence of temperance, chaftity, meeknefs, humility, forbearance, benevolence, beneficence, courtefies? And how different do the unavoidable evils of human life appear, how is their fmart leffened, nay, nearly deftroyed, when the defign of providence in fending them, and their ufes to which they ferve are taken into confideration; when by means of chriftian faith and chriftian hope it becomes the habitual frame of our minds to receive affliction and difappointment, as wholefome medicines to cure the diforders of our fouls, and to promote our great and final good!

DID chriftianity no more than provide fuch a check and remedy for the *evils* of life, it would do a great deal by this very circumftance towards increafing the good: for how open is the mind left by thefe means to every real pleafure which occurs; inftead of being by wrong views fhut againft the admiffion of it; inftead of being, by exceffive indulgences and unfocial conduct, difqualified from enjoying it? But chriftianity does more than this: it gives a higher relifh to every bleffing common to mankind in general, with the addition of peculiar fatisfactions of its own. Your own experience I truft hath taught you far better than any defcription, how much all the comforts and enjoyments of life are increafed, by confidering them as tokens of your maker's love, and earnefts to you of ftill greater bounty; as well as what unalloyed pleafures fpring, from purity of heart, from univerfal charity, from heavenly contemplation, and a well regulated devotion; and above all, from that peace of mind, beyond the power of words to exprefs, which refults from a clear fenfe of the favor of our heavenly Father thro' the merits of our bleffed Redeemer.

If

IF it be the nature of all human satisfactions to pall upon enjoyment, it arises from want of sufficient power in objects which terminate in ourselves, and the boundaries of the present world, to fill all the capacities of an immortal soul, designed by its very nature for a nobler state of existence: but the christian religion by connecting every thing which happens to us in the present life with a future, and forming us to the habit of extending our views in the use of the things of it, beyond ourselves to the glory of God, supplies this natural deficiency, and offers to our minds an object which can never fail. He who has brought himself to look up to his heavenly Father, in every event of his life, with filial love and gratitude, and to consider whatever befalls him, as a part of a gracious plan of probationary education, calling upon him for suitable exertions, will be in little danger of enduring the

miseries

miseries of mental languor or fastidious disappointment.

The only persons exposed to such evils, are they who forget that the pleasures of the present life are sent to soften the calamities of human nature, and the fatigues necessarily attendant upon active pursuits; to smooth our journey through the rugged paths of this world; who look upon enjoyment as the sole end of their being, and consequently, whenever they find it, give themselves up to it without restraint. The christian, by not expecting too much satisfaction from worldly things, escapes the pain of disappointment: by not making the attainment of such satisfactions the chief object of his pursuit, but dividing his attention between these and nobler objects, he prevents the insipidity of languor.

Lastly,

LASTLY, tho' the shortness and uncertainty of this life cannot but be an awful consideration to the mind of man, yet the hopes suggested by christian faith deprives it of all its terrors. For death is a very different object, to him who looks forward to those things which eye hath not seen nor ear heard, nor hath it entered into the heart of man to conceive, from what it commonly appears to the unhallowed view of worldly men: it is a sleep from which he will awake to the glorious dawn of eternal life: it is the end and consummation of all his labour, and will conduct him to the abodes of peace and never fading joy. This world while it lasts is his present portion, and therefore, like a wise man, he makes the most of the satisfactions it affords; but he considers it only as a small earnest of a nobler inheritance which will never decay. And whilst he, whose thoughts have been confined to the objects of this passing scene, trembles at the approach of the great conqueror of human nature; the chriftian can behold him without difmay, and addrefs him in the infpired language of the records of his faith,—O death where is thy fting! O grave where is thy victory! He knows that he *muſt* die, and (without affecting to be above the common apprehenfions of his nature,) he exults at the approach of death, from a perfuafion that it will be to him a paſſage to a joyful refurrection, and a glorious immortality. The time and manner of his death, as all his other concerns, he humbly fubmits to the difpofal of his gracious Father. Who would not wifh to be in fuch a ftate? Who would not wifh to be a chriftian indeed?

If fuch be the real ftate of human nature, and fuch the condition of human life; if fuch a remedy for the diforders of human nature and the evils of human life, be provided

vided in the religion of Jesus Christ; does not a question forcibly recur upon our minds, whether we be using this remedy as we ought? The general effects of christianity in softening men's minds, and enlarging their views ever since its first promulgation, cannot be denied; but fully to answer the ends proposed by it, a thorough and hearty, and steady profession of it, is absolutely necessary.

The times in which we live, and the awful dispensations of providence now carrying on in the world, give peculiar force to the injunction in my text, and in a very affecting manner call us to seriousness and consideration. Amidst many valuable cautions of political prudence, which the dreadful events that have lately taken place in a neighbouring nation, must inculcate on the present and all future generations of mankind; one instruction of much higher importance

portance it is earneſtly to be hoped they will not fail moſt ſtrongly to impreſs on their minds; and that is, that the boaſted attainments of philoſophy and extended knowledge, joined with the higheſt refinement of manners, when not directed by religious principle, leads to greater debaſement of the human character, than a ſtate of ignorance and barbariſm: and that when the revelation of Chriſt has been received amongſt any people, and at length rejected as falſe, every principle of natural religion will be rooted up with it. The people of this country have too much grace, as well as too much good ſenſe, to be in danger of wilfully denying the Lord that bought them: but it behoves us all to conſider, very ſeriouſly, what is the real ſtate of religion amongſt us, I mean, of religion as it is eſteemed by God, who knoweth the ſecrets of our hearts—whether if it be not rejected, it be regarded as it ought; in
ſuch

such a manner as to afford hopes of the continuance of the favor of providence towards this nation, which we have so signally (above all the nations upon earth) experienced through a long period of time.

At least, each member of the Church of England, is particularly called upon at this season to consider well the way in which he is proceeding through life; consideration can do no harm—judge for yourselves: inquire carefully where your true happiness lies, and having discovered it, examine whether you are indeed in the way that leads to it. Look within yourselves, and consider your nature and what it requires; look without you, and consider the world and how it passes on: then look into the gospel of Jesus Christ, and consider what it promises, and how exactly suited it is to your nature and your condition. Do not view the christian religion with an eye of suspicion,

picion, as if it was an enemy to pleasure: it debars not men from any real permanent satisfaction; it would only teach them to draw their pleasures from fountains which will never fail, and which will never send forth bitter waters; pleasures adapted to the whole of their nature, and to its various parts in just subordination: by means of which, they may have the greatest possible enjoyment, attended with the fewest evils in the present life; and in the next, from the perfection of their nature, and the merits of their Redeemer, unmixed, eternal, increasing bliss.

SERMON

SERMON XII.

EPHESIANS, *Ch.* iv. *V.* 14.

"THAT HENCEFORTH, WE BE NO MORE CHILDREN, TOSSED TO AND FRO, AND CARRIED ABOUT WITH EVERY WIND OF DOCTRINE."

THE prefent world, being defigned for a ftate of probation, is fo conftituted as to furnifh a continual fucceffion of events, adapted to exercife the affections, and to give fcope to the powers of the underftanding. In the conduct and regulation of this important faculty, (the moft excellent of God's gifts to man, the tenure by which he holds his fovereignty over the reft of the creation,

creation, and by which he is rendered capable of virtue, and of the rewards annexed to it,) no inconsiderable part of his trial consists: to search patiently for truth, to weigh the pretensions of discordant opinions, and to determine with impartiality as the scale preponderates, is the duty of every one in proportion to his capacity and opportunities of knowledge: but these are so different in different persons, and even in the same person at different periods, that it would betray a very superficial acquaintance with human nature to assert, either that all men must see things in exactly the same light, and draw the same conclusions from them, or that any individual will always necessarily remain in his present sentiments. It is sufficient that in every given conjuncture, he does what conscience dictates, after a fair and full consideration of the case, determining this only, with respect to futurity; that, with God's help, he will then

also

also decide and act as shall appear to be just and right. That peremptory tone, in which so many profess to have made up their minds on the most complex and difficult subjects, proceeds from a mixture of pride and indolence: pride disdains instruction, and revolts from the notion of being kept in the trammels of perpetual childhood; while indolence would fain consider its task as done, and shrinks from the fatigue of new researches, and repeated examination: yet, in proportion as men form a juster estimate of their condition here, they will feel themselves more reconciled to the humiliation of persevering labour, and pregressive knowledge.

There is no affinity between that ingenuous diffidence which keeps the mind always open to conviction, and the wavering state of irresolution which it was the Apostle's intention to condemn. Sincere

and

and sober inquirers after truth are aware that they are liable to be biassed by the suggestions of interest and prejudice, or to be misled by sophistry and false representations; that their views of things are neither clear nor extensive; that many circumstances, essential to a right judgement, may, for the present at least, lie beyond their sphere of observation, or be overlooked, though they lie within it. If the subject of their inquiry admits of demonstration, they are careful to acquaint themselves with the whole of the proof; for even demonstrable truths, may be so plausibly controverted, as to perplex and stagger those who have merely taken them on trust. If it is only capable of probable evidence, (a distinction referable to the fallibility of the human understanding, and not to the nature of truth; which, under whatever denomination, is in itself alike absolute and one;) probability implies, in the very notion of it, that there

are

are prefumptions on the oppofite fide. They advance therefore with cautious fteps; and if, notwithftanding their care, their judgement is unfortunately mifled, no falfe fhame induces them to perfevere; for next to avoiding error, their object is to difcover and correct it: yet they do not refign opinions adopted after mature reflection, and on the fulleft information they were able to obtain, without a fcrupulous examination of what is alleged againft them, and of what is propofed to be fubftituted in their place. On the other hand, the turn of mind that caufes men to be feduced by every fpecious argument, caufes them to be equally ftartled by every fpecious objection.

OPINIONS haftily and confidently taken up, and for a time maintained with the greateft pofitivenefs, are often in the end relinquifhed with as little reafon as they were embraced. Thofe which fucceed to them

them are again displaced by others; till the mind becomes irritable, from finding nothing but confusion, where it had hoped that it rested in certainty; and instead of imputing its disappointment to the real cause, fondly concludes, that what it has failed itself to discover, either has no existence, or is unattainable by human sagacity. Then ensues a torpidity eventually fatal to its powers, which, as is well known, are strengthened and improved by a proper exertion of them, but impaired by inaction, and corrupted by abuse, till the ability of forming just determinations is entirely lost: nor is such a state of mind less destructive, in its consequences, of the best emotions of the heart, than it is of the powers of the understanding. Men come by degrees to think it of little importance whether their notions are right or wrong, and give up indolently whatever the petulance of bold objectors may prompt them to require. Instead

stead of thinking it their duty to contend for the faith which was once delivered to the saints, they begin to doubt whether any faith was ever so delivered, or, at least, think it so uncertain what that faith was, that they see its most essential doctrines attacked and treated with scorn, without uneasiness.

Instability of principle, of whatever kind, is followed by a correspondent instability of conduct; men may act right by chance from the impulse of the moment, or the remains of a disposition intended by nature to be good, but, when situations occur to put them to the test, it will appear that, without a just estimate of the condition of human life, and a well founded conviction of its great and ultimate purpose, the performance either of social or religious duties is very precarious.

In this, as in other instances, nothing is more conducive to a right frame of mind than an awful sense of God's constant presence and inspection. A notion true in itself, when rightly understood, and fairly interpreted, (that men are not responsible for their speculative opinions, nor for the fluctuations to which they are subject from time to time, because opinions depend on evidence, in the reception of which the mind is necessarily passive,) serves often, by the misapplication of it, to lull the conscience in a false security. In that day when the secrets of all hearts shall be open, and every evasion and subterfuge unavailing, it may, alas! be no justification of a mispent life to allege, however truly so, at such and such a period I acted, for so I believed. Practice and belief reciprocally influence each other; and as erroneous belief has often a tendency to produce immoral conduct, so it often originates in it, and is

therefore

therefore reprehenfible in itfelf. In no inftance do men betray greater weaknefs than in accommodating their faith to their habits and propenfities. Is it foothing to believe that remiffion of fins, and even indulgencies for the commiffion of them, may be obtained from men divinely authorifed to difpenfe them; that fome perfons, reprobated from their birth, are children of perdition, while others are fanctified by an over-ruling grace, and predeftined to everlafting happinefs; that certain outward acts of mortification, that enthufiaftic fervors, or unintelligible pretenfions to an extatic love of their Redeemer, will be accepted as equivalent to a life of piety and virtue? The moft frivolous argument, the firft detached paffage that can be interpreted in conformity with the favorite tenet, is confidered as conclufive evidence. Should change of circumftances at any time render fome other creed more convenient, little ingenuity

genuity will be neceffary to detect the errors of their prefent perfuafion, or to find reafons, at leaft equally cogent with thofe on which it was founded, in fupport of the new one. And as fuch repeated changes of fyftem imply a confeffion of the futility of all but the laft, it is not probable that this when affailed in its turn, whether by argument or by the paffions, will be more pertinaciouſly maintained; efpecially if it be confidered that, as by difcarding each particular fet of doctrines fome one fcruple has been quieted; fo by difcarding them all, the very ground of fcruples will be removed; and, in fact, no tranfition is eafier than, from having fucceffively believed every thing, to believing nothing.

Nor are indolence and indifference lefs adverfe than vice to fettled and confiftent plans of thinking or acting. When opinions are acquiefced in, not from a conviction of their

their truth, but to save the trouble of examination, they will be as readily resigned to save the trouble of defending them; indeed from incapacity to defend them, supposing them to be accidentally right. To an indolent mind any system or any objection will appear plausible for the moment; but which of them, or whether any of them, is supported by the degree of evidence which constitutes proof or probability, it neither knows, nor has ever even considered in what that degree of evidence consists.

Such is the imperfection of the human understanding, so unaccountable at times are its misconceptions, arising either from peculiar habits of thinking, or from something which we cannot explain in its original constitution, so strong are the biasses which it is liable to receive in early life from examples and education, that errors arising from these causes are sure to find the

most

moſt equitable, the moſt indulgent allowances from him who knoweth whereof we are made. But the obligations of virtue, the importance of right notions concerning God and their own relation to him, and conſequently the obligation men are under to avail themſelves of every means of information on theſe ſubjects which he may vouchſafe to afford to them, are among the firſt principles of natural religion. All are apprized of them, it depends on themſelves to act ſuitably to them, and would they but bear in mind that they are even now, though leſs ſenſibly, yet not leſs actually in his preſence, than they ſhall be when they are called on to render account of the talents committed to them; that he now ſees, as he ſhall then enquire, whether they ſeek the truth with their whole heart, and carefully abſtain from all known ſin, which is the ſureſt obſtacle to perceiving it, they will then undoubtedly diſcover in all
points

points essential to salvation, and hold fast without wavering, that true, and perfect, and acceptable will of God.

It may not, however, be superfluous to add, that, in the prosecution of every subject which requires serious investigation, it is important to possess just ideas of the powers and deficiencies of human reason. Man comprehends no part of nature thoroughly, and in all its details. Of the principle of cohesion in solid substances, or of life in organized bodies; of the attracting force that pervades the planetary system; of the sympathetic union between the material and immaterial parts of his own constitution, he has not any, not even the obscurest notion. Yet, that such principles exist is attested by their effects beyond the possibility of contradiction. And not only is their existence ascertained, but the laws by which they act have been assigned on such

such just grounds of probability, that nothing less than the production of facts manifestly inconsistent with them, or the failure of consequences that must have resulted from them, had they been true, can be allowed to set them aside. Here the wisest philosophers have stopped, or, if in any instance they have been tempted further, have proposed their sentiments with the diffidence that becomes conjecture. But when, passing these limits, man would penetrate the inmost recesses of nature, and explain, not only the actual connection of causes and effects, but the mode in which her mysterious operations are conducted, the means of conviction fail him; he must address his theories to the imagination, not to the understanding; it is well if he can render them intelligible: sooner or later the perplexity and difficulties that attend them will be pointed out by some ingenious rival, who has, perhaps, new ones still ftill more exceptionable to propofe. By fuch unfuccefsful attempts the credit of what is fufficiently proved is weakened in the minds of thefe, and they are always the greater number, who do not carefully diftinguifh the limit at which evidence ceafes, and conjecture begins.

The fame general principles are applicable to the conduct of philofophical and of religious inquiries: the contents of the book of revelation are intelligible in the fame degree with thofe of the book of nature: in many points indeed the contents of both are the fame; fuch parts of the fyftem of the divine œconomy, as were collected by the fages of antiquity from obfervation and reflection, are confirmed as far as they extend by the teftimony of fcripture: there are other points which we know from that teftimony alone; that the love of Chrift, confpiring with the love of God

God towards mankind, procured the pardon of sins, (a dispensation in which the wisdom of the means is as conspicuous as the benevolence of the end, since no other can be conceived so conducive to the promotion of virtue:) that as man is redeemed by the Son of God, he is sanctified by the Spirit of God, if he avails himself of the means prescribed for obtaining that holy influence. It is not necessary, however, to enumerate the doctrines of this class; they will readily occur to persons at all conversant in the sacred writings, and it is to such persons only that the present argument can be addressed; but it may be observed of them in general, that the authenticity of the volume in which they are delivered is supported by the strongest testimony, and by testimony of that kind of which reason is competent to judge; that they appear, considered with respect to their final causes, replete with wisdom, and worthy of their author;

author; that there is nothing in them contradictory to the cleareſt notions men have of phyſical or of moral poſſibility, nor inconſiſtent with any other part of the plan of providence. On the contrary, the more accurately things are examined in this view, the more harmonious and beautiful does the ſyſtem appear; but when the preciſe nature of the union between the divine perſons concerned in our redemption, or the preciſe mode and degree in which the graces of the holy ſpirit are communicated (and many inſtances of the ſame kind may be ſelected among the doctrines of natural, as well as of revealed religion;) is purſued through the labyrinth of metaphyſical ſubtlety, doubts ariſe, and cavils are objected; to which the true anſwer is, that other faculties than thoſe which we poſſeſs at preſent are neceſſary to diſcover, and probably to conceive, an adequate ſolution of them. But the pride of human ſagacity prompts men to devife one, which being found infufficient, recourfe is had to another and another: what is thus inferted with felf-complacency, is propagated with zeal; and hence have arifen no inconfiderable number of the herefies and fects which have difgraced chriftianity from the days of the Apoftles to the prefent time. The fame overweening opinion of their own difcernment leads men ultimately to difcard as falfe, what is partially obfcure; while yet they allow, with refpect to the infinity of fpace and duration, that it is as impoffible to diveft the mind of the idea, as it is to comprehend or explain it.

THAT the love of truth fhould fometimes be facrificed to the love of eafe, or the judgement be warped by vicious propenfities, is rather matter of concern than of furprife, fince the ftrength of thefe propenfities is evinced by daily experience: but

but it is wonderful that, in purfuits with which the moſt important intereſts are connected, reaſon ſhould frequently be miſled by the mere illuſions of vanity. There are, however, perſons who value themſelves on a certain refinement and ſubtlety of genius, who affect in every ſubject of their inquiry to diſcover what paſſes unnoticed and unſuſpected by men of groſſer apprehenſions; or to find occaſion of doubt and perplexity where a plain underſtanding finds none. The great eſſential principles of religion, as might be expected in a ſyſtem deſigned to conduct all mankind to ſalvation, are ſo revealed as not to be eaſily miſunderſtood: but the perſons in queſtion would think it a diſparagement to their ſagacity, were they to ſee any thing in the ſame light in which it appears to others. Allegorical, figurative, myſtical interpretations are deviſed; and, groundleſs as they are, they are ſure to attract admirers and followers; for

for there is a vanity fo humble as to give itfelf credit for adopting thofe fingularities which it has not ingenuity to invent.

It was far from the intention of the Apoftle, it is far from the intention of this difcourfe, to difcourage the detection of real errors, or to diffuade men from renouncing them. But for the light diffufed by the revival of learning, and the fpirit of the firft reformers, men would have remained under the delufions of Romifh fuperftition, and the bondage of Papal tyranny; and, though Chriftianity was freed at that period from the groffer corruptions with which ignorance and ambition had contributed to debafe it, it is readily acknowledged that there ftill may be paffages of fcripture which are mifapprehended, and that the beft religious eftablifhments partake of that imperfection to which every thing human is liable. To rectify fuch mifapprehenfions is

the

the nobleſt office of criticiſm; to ſupply defects, and to remedy abuſes in ſuch eſtabliſhments is admirable, if what is propoſed to be gained on one hand is not balanced, perhaps exceeded, by ſome diſadvantage on the other. But when (as perſons of a miſanthropic turn conceive that they ought to ſuſpect every man of being an enemy, whom they do not know to be a friend) certain philoſophers lay down for a maxim that each individual ſhould conſider every perſuaſion as falſe till the truth of it has been proved to his particular conviction, and reject every ſyſtem as erroneous till he has ſeen its excellence demonſtrated, the maxim is either inſidious, or formed without ſufficient attention to the actual circumſtances of a great majority of mankind. Every prejudice, it is ſaid, is an impediment in the ſearch of truth: as an abſtract principle this is readily admitted; ſhall parents therefore ſcruple to interpoſe authority to check

the

the wayward paſſions of their children, and leave their minds in a ſtate of neutrality between vice and virtue, till their faculties can diſcover, or at leaſt can thoroughly comprehend, what it is that conſtitutes the eſſential difference between right and wrong? A ſimilar queſtion may be aſked reſpecting religious notions. If while men's tempers and occupations continue ſuch as they are, we ſuppoſe that the generality, left to themſelves, would attain a belief of the exiſtence, attributes, and moral government of God; we ſuppoſe at leaſt as much as would be likely to happen. Is it then deſirable that they ſhould conſider revelation as a fable till they have opportunity to diſcuſs it in detail; or that they ſhould truſt for the evidence of its origin, and the interpretation of the obſcurer parts of it, to perſons whoſe integrity they have no reaſon to ſuſpect, and who are qualified by abilities and learning to give them information?

In

In a nation of philosophers it might be matter of indifference whether, previously to the confideration of a fyftem, they had believed it to be true or falfe: but it is not fo with the bulk of mankind. Let an uninformed perfon fuppofe the chriftian faith, or the external modification of it, profeffed by the fociety to which he belongs, to be indefenfible, and he will foon find, or be furnifhed with, plaufible objections to it. In proportion as a fubject is extenfive and important, it is affailable by ridicule and fophiftry, or by arguments which, though of no real moment, yet, being directed againft that degree of ignorance which is infeparable from a finite underftanding, cannot be fo fatisfactorily anfwered as to preclude the poffibility of farther cavil. Befides, a partial anfwer, however decifive of any fingle point, would be deemed infufficient by one who difbelieved the whole. To be convinced, he muft proceed regularly

through

through the whole body of proof by which the syſtem is ſupported; but to do this, and to appreciate its validity, is probably a taſk beyond his inclination, or his powers.

Those, on the contrary, (it is ſtill the ſame claſs of people that is intended) who reſolve to continue in the things that they have learned and been aſſured of, till they ſee reaſon to think they have been deceived, are not therefore to be accounted ſlaves of prejudice. They will, indeed, ſeek for ſolutions of difficulties that are propoſed to them; they will apply to perſons more enlightened than themſelves, and be ſhewn, perhaps, that objections which ſtartled them were merely ſpecious, or that by a change, which might extricate them from one difficulty, they would be involved in many: yet, where both parties are heard, truth will ultimately prevail; and, let the conteſt be conducted in the faireſt manner, it is no

inconſiderable

inconsiderable advantage on the side of the assailant, that he chooses his point of attack.

THIS concurrence with received opinions, till sufficient cause appears to dissent from them, is recommended with no interested views, but from a sacred love of truth, and as a principle, which, previously to any experiment, and on a mere consideration of the constitution of the human mind, seems likeliest to produce full and impartial discussion. Scenes, which for some years past have filled Europe with horror, attest but too well the tendency of a contrary procedure. Politicians, who would fain persuade you that their distinctive characteristic is benevolence, endeavoured to impress the people with a notion, which in substance, if not in words, was this; whatever is, is wrong; they foresaw, but were not deterred by, the atrocities that followed. They did not foresee that the public mind, fet afloat, would reft in nothing; and that the fabricks they had reared would fo fuddenly follow that which they had deftroyed. They have, however, afforded a leffon to thofe, who, being fincere believers, are at the fame time enthufiaftical in making profelytes to their particular fect; that while they explode and vilify, in the mafs, the particular notions which men of other perfuafions have been accuftomed to cherifh, they make them liable to be toffed to and fro with every wind of doctrine, and to terminate in abfolute infidelity.